DISCARDED

Films About Jewish Life and Culture

FILMS ABOUT JEWISH LIFE AND CULTURE

Michael Taub

Studies in the History and Criticism of Film
Volume 10

The Edwin Mellen Press
Lewiston•Queenston•Lampeter

Library of Congress Cataloging-in-Publication Data

Taub, Michael.
 Films about Jewish life and culture / Michael Taub.
  p. cm. -- (Studies in the history and criticism of film ; v. 10)
 [Includes bibliographical references.]
 ISBN 0-7734-6121-3
 1. Jews in motion pictures. I. Title. II. Series.

PN1995.9.J46F53 2005
791.43'652924--dc22

2005047973

This is volume 10 in the continuing series
Studies in the History and Criticism of Film
Volume 10 ISBN 0-7734-6121-3
SHCF Series ISBN 0-7734-9734-X

A CIP catalog record for this book is available from the British Library.

Copyright © 2005 Michael Taub

All rights reserved. For information contact

The Edwin Mellen Press
Box 450
Lewiston, New York
USA 14092-0450

The Edwin Mellen Press
Box 67
Queenston, Ontario
CANADA L0S 1L0

The Edwin Mellen Press, Ltd.
Lampeter, Ceredigion, Wales
UNITED KINGDOM SA48 8LT

Printed in the United States of America

Dedication

I dedicate this book to my children, Simon and Gideon, for the happiness they bring to my life. I hope they too will love good movies as much as I do.

Table of Contents

Preface by Dr. Alan Berger i
Acknowledgments iii
Introduction iv
"Hester Street" to "Crossing Delancey": Greeners in Hollywood Films 1
The Longest Hatred: Hollywood Confronts Antisemitism 23
Black Hats on the Silver Screen: Religious Life in America 35
Spinoza Confronts the Rabbis: An Israeli Film and Play 45
Romance and Rambos: Hollywood and the Jewish State 55
Major Shoah Films, or When the Exception is the Rule 69
Minor Shoah Films: Fun and Games Allowed 85
Jewish Wedding Bells: Hollywood 2000 Style 101
Appendix 113
Select Bibliography and Filmography 114
Fiction Feature Films and Some Documentaries 117

Preface

There are many books about Judaism and many works dealing with cinematic portrayals of Jewish life. The genius of Michael Taub's study is the author's insightful blending of the two. He writes as an insider, one whose language skills, knowledge of the multifaceted dimensions of Judaism, and thoughtful reflections on Judaism and cinema make this work an essential study. Taub writes with clarity and insight about various dimensions of Jewish life and culture as they are portrayed in film. His discussion ranges from antisemitism to the Holocaust, and from the religious life of American Jews to Hollywood's representation of Israel. And yet the author, himself, writes that "a great film about any aspect of the Jewish experience is yet to be made."

This study skillfully negotiates several key tensions. There is, first of all, the tension between the particularity of Jewish life and culture, and the allure of assimilation as seen in "Avalon." Yet, the reader will also learn much about Jewish intramural tensions. In the struggle between orthodoxy and secularism, Hollywood has chosen to present orthodox figures as more than mere uni-dimensional caricatures. There is as well the tension between the history of the establishment of the Jewish State and its sentimentalized cinematic accounts. Perhaps the most troubling of these tensions concerns the problematics of Holocaust representation. Taub's insightful discussion of "Sophie's Choice," "Europa, Europa," and "Schindler's List" provides the parameters of the limits of such representation whose transgression is the equivalent of blasphemy.

Taub's fascinating discussion of Baruch de Spinoza, the seventeenth-century heretic, reveals much about the tension which suffuses all the works under discussion.

Focusing on two Israeli works, Joshua Sobol's play, "Solo leSpinoza," and Ygal Bursztyn's film, "Everlasting Joy," Taub ilustrates the eternal tension between history and its artistic representation. Sobol's Spinoza emerges as a tragic figure whereas Bursztyn's protagonist appears in a comedy film. The historic Spinoza was neither tragedian nor clown.

Integrating the insights of literary and cinematic criticism, Taub's discussions reveal both the promise and the pitfalls inherent in Hollywood's portrayal of Jews and Judaism. As an astute cultural critic, Michael Taub recognizes that reading is fast becoming a lost art. Large numbers of people derive their notion of reality from films. Yet men and women from the beginning of time have utilized the plastic and, subsequently, visual arts to represent their hopes and fears, dreams and nightmares.

This is one reason why Taub insists on holding cinematic representation of Jewish life and culture to high standards. If cinema is the new "text" of Judaism, this book is an important contribution to the work of interpreting and understanding that text.

Alan L. Berger
Boca Raton, November 2004

Alan L. Berger

Alan L. Berger is Raddock Eminent Scholar Chair of Holocaust Studies and Director of Judaic Studies at Florida Atlantic University. He is the author of, among other works, <u>Crisis in Covenant: The Holocaust in American Jewish Fiction</u> and <u>Children of Job: American Second-Generation Witnesses to the Holocaust</u>.

Acknowledgments

I owe many thanks to people who taught me a great deal about American Jewry: Professor Steven T. Katz, Ellen Schiff and Joel Shatzky.

I am also indebted to Alan Berger, who wrote the Preface. And last, but not least, thank you, Cliff Bailey and Lenny Rogoff, for editing my writing.

Introduction

Jewish life and culture has been the subject of many film makers the world over. Since the early years of Hollywood, American film makers have been bringing to life the remarkable story of the Jewish experience in this country. Their works have considered such important issues as emigration and the formation of ethnic identity, antisemitism, Zionism and Israel, religion and traditional Judaism, and the Holocaust. While the bulk of these essays is about the American Jewish experience, foreign works are also examined because they shed light on issues of interest to Jews everywhere. The chapter, "Spinoza Confronts the Rabbis on Stage and Screen," for example, features two Israeli works dealing with the burning issue of religion versus secularism—a major battle in Israel today—and of great interest to American Jews as well. It is regrettable that important topics like Black-Jewish relations have not yet received serious treatment by American producers.[1]

I would argue that a great film about any aspect of the Jewish experience is yet to be made. We do have some fine works about Hasidic and religious life—"The Chosen" and "A Price Above Rubies"—about the Holocaust—"Schindler's List"—and about immigrants—"Hester Street"—but since the 1947 classic, "Gentlemen's Agreement," Hollywood has not produced one respectable work on

---

[1] On the subject of Black-Jewish relations there is Bernard Malamud's novel, <u>The Tenants</u>, and Herb Gardner's play, "I'm not Rappaport." Several dramas appeared following the 1991 Crown Heights racial disturbances in Brooklyn; Anna Deavere Smith's "Fires in the Mirror" (1993) is the best known.

Tikkun editor, Michael Lerner, and Harvard philosopher and political activist, Cornel West, have held a series of public meetings to start a dialogue between the two communities. To some extent, "The Pawnbroker" (Sidney Lumet, 1965) does touch on this issue, but only lightly.

antisemitism. And, with the exception of the 1960 "Exodus," it has not produced one memorable film on Israel. Finally, as already noted, the film industry has been suspiciously silent on the Black-Jewish front.

Overall, Hollywood has been rather kind to traditional Judaism and Hasidism. Rabbis and Talmudic scholars have generally been treated with reverence. Most films leave viewers with a sense of sadness toward a people and culture virtually wiped out by the Holocaust. This positive (at times even romantic) image has been challenged by Boaz Yakin, the Israeli writer and director of the controversial "A Price Above Rubies." The film's scant exposure, however, seems to indicate the industry's discomfort with promoting works that show the Hasidic community in a bad light. True, Barbra Streisand's "Yentl" is critical of Orthodoxy's discriminatory practices toward women, but, overall, the film paints a flattering picture of Yeshiva life and culture.

While some of today's best fiction by such renowned Jewish-American novelists like Allegra Goodman, Melvin Bukiet, Anita Diamant and Rebecca Goldstein deal with the role of tradition in a secular world, American cinema has yet to tackle this issue seriously.[2] Recent films such as "Keeping the Faith," "Deconstructing Harry" and "Kissing Jessica Stein" do touch on this but, as I show in my "Jewish Weddings Hollywood 2000 Style," only superficially.

---

[2]The literary works I have in mind are: Allegra Goodman's Katerskill Falls; Rebecca Goldstein's The Mind-Body Problem, Strange Attractors, and Mazel; Tova Reich's The Jewish War; and Dani Shapiro's Slow Motion. Most of Chaim Potok's novels deal with religion and modernity as well. A well made Canadian film, "The Quarrel" (Eli Cohen, 1991), addresses issues of religion and secularism in a modern world.

Ran Gilboa's "After All, There Is Something New in Acco," (in Hebrew), "Hair," October 10, 1990 (translation is mine). The 1996 New York production at "LaMama" has been reviewed by Alisa Solomon, "Sympathies Swaying," The Village Voice (December 3, 1996), and by Irene Backalenick, "Masked Men," Back Stage (November 8-14, 1996).

Understandably, Israeli films have been tackling this problem for a long time. Ygal Bursztyn's "Everlasting Joy : The Life and Adventures of Baruch Spinoza," is one artistic example of what happens when secular forces challenge the Orthodox authorities in Israel. America's Jews are, naturally, in a different position from that of their Israeli brothers, but they too are frustrated with Orthodox Judaism's attempts at dominating Jewish life, especially religious practices.[3]

Israel and Zionism are dealt with in the early 1960s with "Exodus" and "Cast a Giant Shadow." In them, Israel's fight for independence is shown as a classic conflict between the forces of good and evil. The Shoah plays a major role in both: above all, it serves as moral justification for Jewish claims to the disputed land. The national drama parallels the personal drama: lovers, one Israeli and one American, are caught up in the madness of the war. This formula explains, in part, the enormous success of these two early American films: without a love story and popular actors like Kirk Douglas and Paul Newman, no one knows how far they would have gone. Interest in the Jewish state resurfaces in the late 1970s following the daring 1976 rescue operation of a hijacked airliner at Entebbe, Uganda. The films are filled with a sense of pride in Jewish power and courage; they glorify the image of the free, nearly superhuman Jew in Israel, the antithesis of the humiliated, helpless creature of a thousand years of European history.

Unlike Israel, immigration has received a fair amount of attention from Hollywood producers. Jewish film makers, some sons and daughters of immigrants

---

[3]Israel has been embroiled in religious wars since the early days. Things, however, got out of hand in the past few decades as Orthodoxy and Hasidism grew in power, much of it thanks to heavy American support. Israeli film makers have been documenting the tensions between secular and religious Jews in: "Halahaka" ("The Band,"1997); "119 Bullets and Three" (1996); and "Longing" (Amalia Margolin, 1998). Feature films such as "Kaddosh" (Amos Gitai, 1999) and "Time of Favor" (Joseph Cedar, 2000) have shown the conflicts between the religious and secular camps, and the dangers of rising religious fanaticism.

themselves, have offered a variety of cinematic images of what it was to be a newcomer or child of a newcomer to America. "Hester Street," "Avalon" and "Crossing Delancey" feature immigrants who came in the great waves of the early part of the century; "Enemies, A Love Story" and "Lost in Yonkers" focus on those who came in the wake of Nazism and in the aftermath of the Shoah. While "Hester Street," "Crossing Delancey" and "Enemies, A Love Story," pay a great deal of attention to the role of Judaism and tradition in the lives of these newly-arrived Americans, "Avalon" and "Lost in Yonkers" create the impression that such concerns were insignificant. It appears that these attempts at universalizing the immigrant experience are designed to widen these films' box office appeal. "Goodbye, Columbus" and "Portnoy's Complaint," two films based on Philip Roth's popular novels, are also important because they show how ethnicity was shaped by a certain type of Jewish mentality typical of first and second generation Jewish immigrants.

While antisemitism is an important factor in most films about Jews, a few have actually adopted it as their main theme. In a sense, Elia Kazan's 1947 classic, "Gentleman's Agreement," is to antisemitism what Joan M. Silver's 1975 "Hester Street" is to immigration: both are yardsticks by which others of the same genre have been judged. Jewish film makers, beginning with the Hollywood moguls of the 1920s and 1930s, have generally been reluctant to tackle this sensitive issue in American society. While recognizing the need to speak out, they were concerned with what it would do to their image. Determined to become part of mainstream America, "one of the boys" so to speak, the last thing they wanted was to be viewed as outsiders, critics of a system that has brought them success and power beyond the wildest imagination of Jews elsewhere in Diaspora.

To solve the problem, they devised a clever formula. It is true that antisemitism exists, and it is our duty to eradicate it; however, we should not simply fight it because it is wrong to discriminate against Jews, but because it is bad for everyone. Allowing injustice toward one minority group, they suggested, makes it possible for a whole host of other injustices to flourish, and no one can be sure whom the next target will be. It should be mentioned that some Woody Allen films do tackle, albeit superficially, and in a humorous way, the phenomenon of antisemitism; "Annie Hall" (1987), "Deconstructing Harry" (1998) and, more recently, "Anything Else," (2003) are some good examples. Finally, "State and Main," a recent work by David Mamet (2000), touches on hatred toward Jews, but, unfortunately, it is only a side issue in the film. Unfortunately, most of my essays have been written before some of the more recent titles came on to the screen.

For the last half century, America and the world have been trying to cope with the memory and legacy of the Shoah. Jewish communities around the world are responsible for creating a variety of projects and programs involving Holocaust education in schools and colleges. American Jews have generously funded the building of major museums like The Simon Wiesenthal Center in Los Angeles, The US Holocaust Memorial in Washington DC, and The Museum of Jewish Heritage: A Living Memorial to the Holocaust in New York.[4]

Telecasts like the 1959 classic documentary, "Judgement at Nurenberg," and the 1978 NBC series, "Holocaust," helped raise consciousness about the Shoah.

---

[4]The enormous support for Holocaust projects (as compared to Israel or Yiddish-related projects) in this country has drawn some criticism. Some claim that the Shoah has become the new "religion" for too many American Jews. Shoah studies are now mandated in many states. There are several academic chairs in Holocaust studies, as well as undergraduate and graduate programs. Holocaust films are hotly debated in the Jewish community and in the general media. Classic examples are "Schindler's List" and the highly controversial "Life is Beautiful." Issues such as the Vatican and the Shoah, the recently discovered wartime Swiss bank accounts of Shoah victims, and the dispute over looted art belonging to Jewish families, are covered extensively by leading newspapers and analyzed in depth by prestigious journals. One of the fiercest critics of the American exploitation and commercialization of the Shoah is Norman Finkelstein. His book on the subject is The Holocaust Industry (2000).

Feature films like "Sophie's Choice" (1982), "Europa, Europa," (1991), "Schindler's List" (1993), Roberto Benigni's "Life is Beautiful" (1998), Roman Polanski's "The Pianist" (2002), as well as the publication of numerous memoirs, diaries and novels, have made the Shoah an integral part of mainstream American culture. While great cinematic achievements, these films are, by no means, flawless. By dealing with bizarre and exceptional occurrences or, as in the case of "Life is Beautiful," the comical and surreal, these works fall short of telling the real Shoah story. For that we must view Claude Lanzmann's nine hour documentary, "Shoah," or many other fine non-fiction works. Lesser known Holocaust films, such as "Apt Pupil" (1999) and "The Devil's Arithmetic" (1999), are meant to educate the young on the lessons of the Holocaust. Unfortunately, they are too contrived, too cliche-ridden to have the desired effect.

A final word on Woody Allen, and why none of his films are included in these discussions. While I enjoy most of his work, Allen, as I mentioned before, has yet to make a film that confronts, as the main theme, a particular Jewish issue. As everyone knows, throughout his long and distinguished career, he has repeatedly parodied Jewish religion, Jewish families and Jewish mothers. In one of his latest efforts, "Deconstructing Harry," he lashes out against religious revival, through, no less, a character played by Demi Moore, the perennial sex symbol.[5]

Writing about a cultural phenomenon in progress is risky business. New and different screen works appear every year. This means that we might have to revise our thinking accordingly. I expect American Jewish directors, such as Woody Allen,

---

[5]Jews and Jewishness are present in some of Allen's earlier works: "Bananas" (1971); "Annie Hall" (1977); and "Manhattan" (1979). Of more recent titles, "Hannah and Her Sisters" (1986), "Radio Days" (1987), "Deconstructing Harry" (1997) and "Anything Else" (2003) are, arguably, the most "Jewish" of his works. Of course, every time Allen plays himself in a particular role, Jewishness is a factor.

Steven Spielberg, Paul Mazursky, Barbra Streisand, and others, to keep making films of Jewish interest. I trust someone will eventually tackle the Black-Jewish problem, Jewish tradition and homosexuality, and the role of American Jews in a post-Zionist world.

More American viewers should be exposed to the excellent work of contemporary European and Israeli directors whose prospective on things is very different from their American counterparts.[6] With the fall of communism, new opportunities present themselves in Central and Eastern Europe. The tragic story of Russia's two million Jews under Stalin and subsequent Soviet dictators has yet to be told. With the borders and archives open for all, such projects are no longer impossible.

---

[6]Most major North American cities schedule a yearly Jewish film festival. These events are great opportunities to view new works by European and Israeli artists. It is impossible to single out any number of films from the output of this international group without doing injustice to those left out. The following titles are only intended to illustrate variety, not quality or personal preference. The German-Russian film, "Lovers in Minsk: The Jewess and the Captain" (Ulf von Mechow, 1994), describes a love story between a Nazi officer and a Jewish woman; a Dutch film, "Left Luggage" (Jeroen Krabbe, 1999), about a young Jewish nanny working for an Orthodox family in Antwerp (Isabella Rossellini plays the religious mother!); a British work, "The Governess" (Sandra Godbacher, 1998), follows the adventures of a Jewish Jane Eyre, (Minnie Driver), a woman who leaves London to work for gentiles in a remote Scottish castle, all the while hiding her identity.

Australia's "Russian Doll" (Dir. Stavros Kazantzidis, 2001) is a quirky comedy about two Jewish men (one married) and a sexy Russian who seeks marriage to stay in the country. A world away, in Argentina, we find "Autumn Sun" (Dir. Eduardo Mignogna, 2000), a touching love story between a middle-aged Jewish woman and a Gentile. Finally, the latest is Francois Dupeyron's (2003) "Monsieur Ibrahim," a moving story of friendship between an elderly Muslim (Omar Sharif) and a Jewish boy, in Paris.

Contrary to common perceptions, not all Israeli films deal with politics, war and violence. For example, Michal Bat Adam and Eli Cohen have been creating interesting works on women and women's issues, as has Julia Shles with the highly popular "Tel Aviv Stories" (1991). "Amazing Grace" (Amos Gutman, 1992) is the first Israeli film to deal with the AIDS epidemic. Finally, Shles' "Afula Express" (1997), possibly Israel's best film of the 1990s, is a story about two average people in love, struggling to reach their dreams.

"Hester Street" to "Crossing Delancey":
Greeners in Hollywood Films

Typically, immigrant films deal with the process of merging and gradual assimilation into mainstream America. The similarities, however, end there. While dealing with this central issue, films like "Hester Street" (1975), "Crossing Delancey" (1989) and "Enemies, A Love Story" (1990), do so against the backdrop of the clash between traditional Eastern-European values and modern American values. "Enemies, A Love Story," a screen adaptation of an I. B. Singer story, is somewhat different since it focuses on immigrants who are also Holocaust survivors. While only marginally about immigrants, two Philip Roth adaptations, "Goodbye, Columbus" (1969), and "Portnoy's Complaint" (1972), treat some of the emotional and psychological problems facing second generation immigrants.

In what appears an attempt at universalizing the immigrant experience, works like "Avalon" (1990) and "Lost in Yonkers" (1993) avoid altogether the socio-religious aspects of Jewish immigration; instead, they concentrate on general socio-economic issues facing newcomers of all ethnic backgrounds. Not surprisingly, while the setting for the first group of films is distinctly Jewish—the Lower East Side, Brooklyn, the Bronx, or Jewish suburbia—the plots of the second group appear to unfold in mixed or only vaguely ethnic neighborhoods. In the more "Jewish" works, the ruined world of Eastern-European community life—its traditions and basic old-world values—leaves us feeling a sense of loss, even somewhat nostalgic. For example, in Roth's "Goodbye, Columbus"—a biting satire on assimilation—Aunt Gladys' down-to-earth wisdom and old world values are certainly more endearing than the fake ethnicity of many of the more Americanized characters in both the novel and film version. In the second, less ethnic group of films, a character's European background, his or her experiences before coming to America, is glossed over or seen as something that belongs to another time and place, unsuitable, even a hindrance to survival and success in the New World.

Before discussing the films proper, I will briefly touch on some key issues involved in Jewish immigration. Though Jews have been coming to this continent since the Mayflower, most films deal with the two major waves of immigrants—the early century migration of over a million and a half Eastern-European Jews, and the influx of thousands of Holocaust survivors in the late 1940s.

Most Jewish immigrants, whether coming to America in the big waves of the early decades of the century, or in the aftermath of the Shoah, faced a variety of difficult emotional, social and cultural problems.[1] The early, as well as post-war immigrants, had to contend with the knowledge that once here, their chances of ever seeing the old world again were very slim, practically non-existent. After enduring arduous, long sea voyages, the Jews of the earlier waves were too poor to even contemplate another trip in their lifetime; Shoah survivors—mostly from countries that fell under Communist rule—faced practically sealed borders once becoming American citizens. Italians and Irish, on the other hand, could return to their birthplace, visit family members and friends, as many times as their wallets permitted. On the other hand, only a few new American Jews ever benefitted from this luxury.

Coming from small, close-knit communities, early century East-European

---

[1] The history of Jewish immigration to America is amply documented in a variety of scholarly books by Oskar Handlin, Harry Feingold, Arthur Hertzberg, Moses Rischlin, Jacob Marcus, Jacob Katz and Nathan Glazer. The following books, however, are suitable for a wider readership audience: Irving Howe, World of Our Fathers (New York: Schocken Books, 1989); Abraham Cahan, The Rise of David Levinsky (New York: Harper and Brothers, 1917); and Deborah D. Moore and Paula Hyman, eds., Jewish Women in America (New York: Rutledge, 1998). For analyses of film and television treatments of immigration and Jewish ethnicity, see: Patricia Erens, "Between Two Worlds: Jewish Images in American Films," in Randall M. Miller, ed., The Kaleidoscopic Lens: How Hollywood Views Ethnic Groups (New York: Jerome Ozer Publishers, 1980); Michael Elkin, "The Jews on TV: From the Goldbergs to Hill Street Cops," in Jewish Exponent, June 28, 1985; Vincent Brown, "The Americanization of Molly: How Mid-Fifties TV Homogenized the Goldbergs (and got Berg-larized in the Process)," in Cinema Journal, Summer, 1999.

Jews had to contend with the largely impersonal life-style of big American cities where most of them settled. To ease the transition and help them integrate, they created a variety of social, charitable and cultural organizations, such as the famous *Landsmanshaftn* aid societies, designed to assist people from a particular town or region. Still, a *shtetl* dweller in New York was in a state of shock for months, perhaps years, after arriving in America.[2] Serious emotional difficulties arose from the fact that many newcomers arrived without their immediate families, thus lacking even the most basic emotional support needed to alleviate some adjustment pains. While it is true that what they left behind was widespread economic misery and anti-Semitism, it is also true that a suffering Jew in Europe was rarely alone. As we all know, the tightly-knit communal life of old world, Eastern-European villages and towns always provided some comfort and security to the needy. Most of this was missing in the fast-paced American world of money and success.

The largest concentration of these new Jews was on the Lower East Side of Manhattan which, in 1900, was the largest ghetto in the new world with a population of over a quarter million people, all squeezed into an area of about a dozen city blocks. Jews of all sorts—tailors, sweatshop operators and laborers, pushcart peddlers, and a variety of other small-time merchants—somehow managed to live together, trying very hard to make a living in what they sarcastically called in Yiddish, *di goldene medine*, the "golden land." Pushed together in crowded tenements on rents ranging anywhere between $6 and $8, most immigrants had to live with lack of privacy, disease, noise and poverty. Their dream was to save enough money and one day leave this misery for a better life "uptown."

---

[2]Of all the many charity organizations, the *Landsmanshaftn* were the most popular. See: Michael Weisser, <u>A Brotherhood of Memory: Jewish Landsmanshaftn in the New World</u> (Ithaca: Cornell University Press, 1985).

This crowded place, the setting for the best known film of immigrant life in turn-of-the-century New York, is Joan Micklin Silver's "Hester Street," a universally acclaimed work featuring Carol Kane in the role of Gitl. She is the newly arrived wife of Jake, who has been in New York three years, and, like many green Jews those days, is a machine operator in a sweatshop. The film is based on Abraham Cahan's 1896 novella, Yekl; A Tale of the New York Ghetto.[3]

Jake is a man about town, a man intoxicated with the freedoms America has to offer, particularly the freedom to keep his marital status a secret from Mamie, the voluptuous owner of a dance studio who loves him and occasionally lends him money for rent. Jake (formerly "Yankl") is among those newcomers who takes freedom to mean shaking off the things he brought with him from the old country—language, clothes, customs, but most of all, religious and traditional values. Instead, he wants to look and sound like a "Yankee." This translates to playing with his son a game of that all-American sport—baseball—exploring the outdoors, engaging in physical activity, which, as one critic correctly observed, signifies his escape "not only from persecution by the Russians but also from the oppressive messianic Jewish tradition, with its stress on worthwhile activities . . . a tradition that valued learning above all."[4]

His wife Gitl, on the other hand, undergoes only a few superficial changes: to appease him she starts to dress and wear her hair differently from the way she did in Europe. Unlike Jake, Gitl is rather comfortable with who she is. Instead of abandoning old values, she is determined to preserve them; this includes observing

---

[3] Abraham Cahan, Yekl: A Tale of the New Ghetto (New York: D. Appleton, 1896).

[4] The New Yorker (unsigned film review), November 24, 1975, p. 167. Most critics loved the film; all of them applauded Carol Kane's acting. See: Richard Eder's review in The New York Times, October 20, 1975.

religious customs and continuing to speak Yiddish. She is unimpressed by Jake's bombast of materialistic ambitions; on the contrary, she falls for Bernstein, a poor, unassuming, Talmudic scholar, whom she marries soon after divorcing Jake, the aspiring "Yankee Jew." The way she goes about getting what she wants is full of irony.

It did not take Gitl long to realize that Jake is not the same man, the Yankl, she once married in Europe and had a child with. This man, she soon finds out, is merely interested in himself, in preserving the freedom to continue living his life with Mamie just like he did prior to Gitl's arrival in New York. This not-so-secret "other" woman is flashy and coarse, the exact opposite of Gitl who is modest, timid, in short, a shy greenhorn. But even this shy greenhorn reaches a limit; refusing to be ridiculed anymore, Gitl demands a divorce. Jake thinks she will go quietly. But, as things turn out, Gitl will only agree to a divorce if Jake and Mamie first empty their pockets; in an unexpected turn of events, the timid greenhorn musters enough chutzpah to ask far more than the two more veteran New Yorkers had ever imagined. In the end, as one critic observed, "the timid Gitl, who has been betrayed and humiliated, comes out with the better man, Bernstein. Gitl even gets Mamie's money, and without having to raise her voice."[5] As for Jake, he has no choice but to marry the outraged, outmaneuvered Mamie. In a scene that captures their demise, the penniless couple, instead of riding in style, is forced to walk to City Hall for the civil ceremony.

Has Gitl been sufficiently "Americanized" to pull off this stunt, or is she just plain smart, in a quiet, unassuming, way? Most likely, it is a combination of the two. In any event, with the money she collected, Gitl plans to open a shop, and, like countless shtetl women, she will support Bernstein's study needs. On the one hand,

---

[5] Ibid.

she learns rather quickly how to handle her philandering, bullying husband; on the other, she assumes a role usually associated with traditional, submissive wives. If one act makes her a free, modern woman, the second appears to negate it.

In an essay comparing the film version to the Cahan novella on which it is based, Sanford Marowitz shows how director Silver turns Cahan's "Yekl's story" into "Gitl's story," a remarkable cinematic tale of a traditional, immigrant woman gradually becoming a feminist, a new Jewish woman."[6] In some regards, Gitl is reminiscent of some of the women we meet in the moving autobiographical narratives written by women like Bella Spewack and Anzia Yezierska about life in the early part of the 20th century on the Lower East Side.[7] Most of what we read is about suffering, prostitution, poverty and humiliation. Any woman who broke out of this cycle must have possessed extraordinary courage, talent and intellect. Much as we would like to believe Marowitz about Gitl becoming a "new Jewish woman," I believe there is no reason to be overly optimistic. It is true that in the context of her times, her decision to leave Jake for a man she loves and respects, is indeed remarkable. But her decision to work while Bernstein studies the Talmud indicates that Gitl has some ways to go before becoming a fully "liberated woman."

This rather unconventional plot of love and betrayal among newly arrived Jewish immigrants is set against the background of Lower East Side tenements, the hustle and bustle of street life full of peddlers, beggars, hookers, drunkards, and a whole host of colorful types that once filled this huge Jewish ghetto. To convey the flavor of old world Jews, Silver employs several Yiddish-speaking actors from the

---

[6]Sanford Marovitz, "Hester Street and the Imported Bridegroom," Modern Jewish Studies, No. 11, 1999.

[7]A great source for studying the specifically women immigrant experience is Moore and Hyman's Jewish Women in America (New York: Routledge, 1997).

Yiddish stage. For example, in the *ghet* (divorce) scene, the Rabbi is played by Zvi Skooler, and his wife by Eda Weiss Morin, two veterans of the Yiddish theater. Despite it sounding at times more Germanic than Yiddish, Carol Kane's speech achieves the desired affect of evoking a distant, foreign world. Some signs on shops and buildings are in Hebrew characters, which adds to the ghetto-like atmosphere of the place.

As Cahan and Silver show us, Americanization took on various forms: while Jake is the type who wholeheartedly embraces American culture, Bernstein rejects it, clinging on to old traditions. Gitl, on the other hand, seems to have found a balance between preserving some of the old ways while absorbing new ones. Thus, she makes a concerted effort to continue speaking Yiddish, while learning English; while making sure her son learns secular subjects, she insists on his devoting equal, if not more, time to religious studies and *yiddishkayt*—in general.

While Gitl and Bernstein struggle to preserve old-world values, Izzy, Silver's other Jewish hero in "Crossing Delancey," slowly, though at first reluctantly, returns to these very values. Izzy (Amy Irving) is a 33-year-old single woman, living and working at an uptown Manhattan bookstore. Through her work she meets writers, editors and a host of interesting intellectual types. She has an affair with a married man, but that does not seem to bother this quintessential smart, sophisticated, liberated woman of the 1980s. While we know nothing about her parents, we do, however, meet her *bubby* who still lives on the Lower East Side with a few remaining Eastern-European, Yiddish-speaking old men and women.

Through her *bubby*, Izzy meets Sam (Peter Riegert), a pickle man in this once predominantly Jewish, but now multi-ethnic neighborhood. He is a traditional Jew who runs the family business; he prays every morning, and while familiar with what goes on in the "big world," Sam harbors no desire of leaving the once predominantly

Jewish ghetto for "greener pastures" uptown. As expected, the first meeting between this sophisticated "uptown girl" and the the Lower East Side pickle man, results in failure. Though touched by his integrity, decency and old-world charm, she cannot imagine spending a lifetime with a man from a world so radically different from hers. But as time goes on, Izzy comes to realize that her uptown world of selfish, self-absorbed intellectuals is no longer the only option in her life. As Kathryn Bernheimer observes, "Izzy comes around to recognize the need to connect with her heritage . . . to change her assumptions about his world . . . to see that while adoring, romantic and steadfast, Sam is not about to be taken for a fool. He's direct and decent, qualities we come to appreciate along with Izzy."[8] In a long article on Jews in American films, Terry Barr is even more optimistic about this woman's prospects of reconnecting with her ethnic roots. She argues that in "Crossing Delancey," "Jewish tradition and family ultimately win out, and it seems that Izzy truly follows her heart. She can have a career, a romance and marriage, and Jewish culture too, or at least the film leaves the door open for all three."[9]

In "Hester Street," Gitl gets the better man, Bernstein, a traditional Jew who, unlike Jake and most immigrants, is not so eager to abandon old values for all the promises of America's freedoms and materialism. Nearly a century later, we meet Izzy who has fully benefitted from these promises but is attracted to Sam, a man who knows full well what awaits him on "the other side" but prefers to stay within the "ghetto walls" as it were. Apparently, for Micklin Silver, assimilation tends to produce disenchanted, even slightly confused Jews. While not advocating a full

---

[8] Kathryn Bernheimer, The 50 Greatest Jewish Movies: A Critic's Ranking of the Very Best (Secaucas, NJ: Carol Publishing, 1998), p. 54.

[9] Terry Barr, "Eating Kosher, Staying Closer," Journal of Popular Film and Television, Vol. 24, No. 3, Fall, 1996, p. 143.

return to the narrow world of ghetto life, Silver seems to be suggesting a compromise, a way of life that combines the modern with the traditional, perhaps something akin to what is commonly referred to nowadays as "modern Orthodoxy." Although the time and the setting are different, these two Silver films are filled with nostalgia for the past: the simpler, more virtuous world of our European forefathers, a world corrupted by the fast-paced, materialistic American culture.

This very culture—post-war New York—is the setting for Paul Mazursky's 1989 screen adaptation of I. B. Singer's novella "Enemies, A Love Story." In the "Author's Note," I. B. Singer writes: "This novel is by no means the story of the typical refugee, his life, and struggle. Like most of my fictional works, this book presents an exceptional case with unique heroes and a unique combination of events. The characters are not only Nazi victims but victims of their own personalities and fates. If they fit the general picture, it is because the exception is the rule. As a matter of fact, in literature, the exception is the rule."[10] The unique heroes are Herman Broder (Ron Silver), Masha (Lena Olin), Yadwiga (Margaret Sophie Stein), and Tamara (Angelica Huston), all Holocaust survivors living in 1947 New York.

"The unique combination of events" is the fact that Herman, a Polish Jew, a bookseller and writer, finds himself involved with three wives: Yadwiga, his former maid in Poland who kept him alive during the war by hiding him in a hayloft; Masha, a camp survivor, a sultry, volatile woman, with whom he has a torrid affair while living with Yadwiga; Tamara, the presumed dead wife from before the war, who suddenly turns up and settles on the Lower East Side. Yadwiga wants to convert to Judaism and start a family with Herman; Masha is violently jealous of Yadwiga and wants him to divorce her and live with her instead; Tamara, on the other hand, seems

---

[10]I. B. Singer, "Preface" to Enemies, A Love Story (Greenwich, CT: Fawcett Books, 1972).

to be satisfied with an occasional visit, conversation, and whenever possible, sleeping with him. Between conjugal visits to three boroughs, Herman is trying to make a living traveling to bookstores selling Jewish books and working for a New York rabbi as a ghostwriter on Jewish subjects.

Unlike the immigrants depicted in the other films discussed here, Herman is a well-educated man. But, like many new immigrants, he too must settle for low-paying jobs and endure the humiliation of doing something beneath his intellectual capacity. Unlike many who came to America before him, Herman is not driven by the desire to achieve material success. For this complex man—a survivor haunted by terrifying memories of life in hiding—some sort of emotional fulfillment and peace of mind are more important than money. Among his torments, he suffers recurrent visions and nightmares of barking dogs, drawn guns, and Nazis in hot pursuit. Masha, a high-strung, emotionally damaged survivor, is experiencing torments of her own. There are hints that in the camps she was forced into prostitution.

It appears that in an uncertain world, their wild sexual encounters are, in the words of critic David Danby, "The one thing they trust. It blots out the past and reaches to the future."[11] As survivors with a similar past, they instinctively understand each other, and depend on each other for emotional support. When complications arise and they can no longer maintain their twisted relationship, Masha commits suicide. Granted, Singer/Mazursky are dealing in extremes; nonetheless, Herman and Masha's predicament is symptomatic of a wider problem: during the late 1940s, survivors were treated with a mixture of sympathy, uneasiness and discomfort. While people felt sorry for them, their dark stories of victimization and

---

[11] David Denby, New York Magazine, December 18, 1989.

helplessness clashed with the positive, upbeat culture of post-war America. Some retreated into total silence, worked hard at attaining the American dream, and became successful career or business people. Some, like Singer's strange lovers, fell prey to their inner demons; unlike the socially and economically successful ones, these survivors were social failures, so they clung to each other desperately.[12]

Mazursky sets this typical Singer drama in New York's subways, streets and apartments. The outdoor shots, in Janet Maslin's words, contain "a vibrant glow, but their vitality runs much deeper than that. The thriving Jewish culture that is seen in the background, along busy streets and even in dim, cramped apartment houses, becomes a sign of affirmation in contrast to the characters' terrible memories. . . . Even in the hubbub of Coney Island, the film glimpses a New York filled with enough promise to do battle against the characters' pain."[13] Jewish culture is, in fact, just about everywhere in this film. It is present in the homes of Herman's women, in a packed synagogue where a Yom Kippur service is held, in a rabbi's house, in the Hebrew signs, and in Yiddish conversations. Not all ethnic scenes are serious in this film: what Herman sees at a Catskill resort, where predominantly urban Jews conduct themselves like typical material for *borsht belt* stand-up comics, brings to mind The Apprenticeship of Duddy Kravitz, the 1959 Mordecai Richler book and subsequent film directed by Ted Kotcheff (1974).

The satire is much harsher in "Goodbye Columbus" (Larry Peerce, 1969) and

---

[12] An excellent cinematic depiction of the ambivalence and discomfort greeting survivors in post-war America is the documentary, "A Long Way Home." Recent scholarly works on the Shoah and popular culture also deal with the reception of survivors by Americans. See: Jeffrey Shandler, While America Watches: Televising the Holocaust (New York: Oxford University Press, 1999) and Peter Novick, The Holocaust in American Life (Boston: Houghton Mifflin, 1999).

[13] Janet Maslin, The New York Times, December 13, 1989.

"Portnoy's Complaint" (Ernest Lehman, 1972).[14] Roth's Jews are seen in both urban and suburban settings. While not religious, they do however engage in some basic ethnic/cultural activities such as Temple services, Shabbes dinners, Bar Mitzvahs, and membership in Hadassah and Bnei Brith. These Jews—mostly second-generation immigrants like the Patimkins, the Klugmans and the Portnoys—are simply going through the motions; their acts empty of meaning or substance. In fact, as Roth shows us, they go to Temple services or Bar Mitzvah parties in part to catch up on gossip, make business contacts, meet an important person, or show off a new dress. Of course, urban Jews from Newark are somewhat more authentic than the country-club Patimkins from New Jersey. But, if the Patimkins are any indication, the real religion for these descendants of immigrant Jews is the almighty American dollar.

While parents chase the dollar, the children grow up confused and neurotic. Neil Klugman and Alex Portnoy (Richard Benjamin) are both bright, well educated, socially conscious individuals. But their lives are consumed by guilt, arising from the conflict of meeting the expectations of pushy, often suffocating parents, and the desire to lead one's life as one wishes.

The outcome is disastrous. Neil's life is nearly ruined when he becomes involved with Brenda (Ali MacGraw), a Jew to be sure, but nonetheless the wrong girl for him. She is a spoiled child, but to the blue-collar Neil, she embodies the success he should aspire to. Although he mocks her bourgeois life style and

---

[14]The appearance of these two novels by Roth was greeted by a chorus of complaints from the Jewish establishment. Roth's tearing into tradition and religious themes infuriated so many that he quickly became a cause celebre in the Jewish world. For an in-depth discussion of the public debate generated by these controversial works, see: Jay Halio, Philip Roth Revisited (New York: Twayne Publishers, 1992). In a recent review of Gerald Shapiro's Bad Jews, Elena Lappin writes: "Roth's fearless take on traditional Jewish themes managed to unsettle the more philistine circles of American Jewish establishment." The New York Times, October 17, 1993.

materialistic outlook on things, obtaining her, as Lester Friedman observes, "is a triumph for Neil, a sign that he too has grasped a piece of the American dream through securing Brenda's affections."[15] Alex, the other rebellious son, runs off with the "monkey," the quintessential *shiksa,* every Jewish parent's nightmare! While he cannot marry her (It would kill his parents!), he does with her everything his mother, father, rabbi and teachers said he shouldn't do. Both Neil and Alex are products of excessive parental pressures and success-driven societal forces, partially reflecting the American work ethic. But, to a large degree, the two are the recipients of a whole host of real and imaginary anxieties and insecurities that are part and parcel of any immigrant's inner world.

The immigrant environments depicted by Silver, Mazursky and the two Roth adaptations are unambiguously Jewish; people speak Yiddish, use Jewish expressions, live in Jewish homes, and speak of typical Jewish experiences. By preserving Jewish flavor, these directors are not merely showing the typical struggles of all immigrants and their children—the experiences of a traditional housewife, a pickle merchant, a salesman, a librarian (Neil Klugman), a city government official (Alex Portnoy)—but they also introduce us to the particular ethnic world that characterized the life of these first and second generation Eastern-Europeans on their way to becoming full Yankees.

In contrast to these works where ethnicity is shown to play a major role in the characters' lives, two autobiographical films—"Avalon," a work written and directed by Barry Levinson, and "Lost in Yonkers," a Neil Simon screen version of his play directed by Martha Coolidge—depict Jewishness as something purely external, characterized primarily by speech and mannerisms. Barely identifiable as Jews, the

---

[15]Lester Friedman, The Image of the Jew, p. 213.

heroes of these films are carefully drawn to appear as "new Americans" hailing from somewhere in Europe, but virtually indistinguishable from their Irish or Italian counterparts.

Avalon is a Baltimore neighborhood where on July 4, 1914, Sam Krichinsky (Armin Mueller-Stahl), one of four Polish-Jewish brothers, arrives in America. The film follows 50 years in the life of these brothers and their children, but focuses primarily on Sam's son Jules and his first cousin Izzy, future business partners in Baltimore's first major discount store. For a while the family lives on the same block with Sam and Eva (Joan Plowright) residing in Jules' apartment. Sam's father had arrived in America in 1926; Eva's brother, a Holocaust survivor, thought to be dead, arrives several years after the liberation with his wife and child.

Despite occasional disagreements and some typical family feuds, the Krichinskys manage to stay together in Avalon until the early 1950s when the television age and the mass exit to suburbia radically changes their life. Jules and Izzy head to tree-lined streets outside Baltimore while Sam and Eva leave to join Eva's brother on a New Jersey farm. This is the beginning of the end for the once-tight Krichinsky family clan, a group of colorful first and second generation successful immigrants who eventually pay a heavy price for their economic success. Modern life with TV viewing during dinner, and sprawling, isolated suburban homes, fosters a new type of individual, one who values privacy over communal living, Howdy Doody and Milton Berle over old stories of the Krichinsky family saga.

In this Jewish household, however, the stories are always told over Thanksgiving dinners, not the Jewish holidays. This is a time for the family to reminisce and reflect on what lies ahead, a time for "old timers" to connect with the young. And it is precisely on these occasions that one expects some Jewish content, a hint of ethnic culture. There is surprisingly very little to satisfy our expectations other than the accent of some old timer. Gabriel Krichinsky, played by Lou Jacobi, a veteran of many Jewish roles, keeps saying "toykey" instead of "turkey," "voter" instead of "water." After Jules gets mugged working as a door-to-door salesman, one of the uncles lets out one audible Yiddish word—*umglick* (misfortune). Sam's wife Eva (Joan Plowright) occasionally slides into Yiddish pronunciations as well but, unlike Jacobi who sounds authentic, Plowright sounds fake. Clearly, the man praying for and eulogizing Eva at her funeral near the film's end is a rabbi, but the scene is very brief; the images move very fast, so it is possible to miss the fact that this indeed is a Jewish moment.

Another opportunity for some *yiddishkayt* is when Eva's family arrives from Europe. They are Holocaust survivors who speak only Yiddish and Polish. As expected, the first moments at the train station are filled with hugs and kisses. The dialogue is hardly audible. Only if listening very closely do we hear them saying words like *a mazeldike shu* (literally a lucky hour, meaning "thank God"), *mayne mishpoche* (my family), and *tayere shvester* (dear sister). Another aborted "Jewish moment" is when, instead of speaking in Yiddish, these refugees speak in Polish. And, once again, they do so over a Thanksgiving feast, not a Jewish celebration, which would naturally be much more familiar to them.

During most of the film, these new refugees talk in Polish, mostly about their suffering in the camps. One expects that such horrific stories would leave a mark on the listener. Contrary to reasonable expectations, except for some slight confusion on the part of Jules' and Izzy's wives, very little changes around the Krichinsky household. The two women are unsure about the circumstances surrounding the survivor couple's life—whether the two had met in the camps—and about the circumstances of the birth of their baby. Ironically, their conversation takes place in a kitchen overflowing with food; at the point where the subject of the concentration camps and gas chambers comes up, one of the women gently and carefully shoves a big, dressed-up turkey into the hot oven! The casual chat, however, is abruptly brought to a halt when one of them, cringing, says: "It gives me the creeps." Throughout this scene, however, there is no mention of the fact that the people in these horrible stories, including lost relatives, were Jewish. In fact, it is not at all clear whether the wives of the young Krichinsky brothers are Jews at all. If anything, their looks and demeanor seem to indicate that they are not. Are we to assume that the Krichinskys have strayed and married gentiles?

Somehow, Levinson's ambiguous or understated ethnicity went unnoticed by most critics. Georgia Brown of The Village Voice did, however, wonder why a Jewish director shooting such a rich slice of ethnic life about his own family of immigrants is so vague about ethnicity. Why, asks Brown, is Levinson "so fastidiously general about religion."[16] I think Levinson is "fastidious" because he wants to portray a group of immigrants as "all-American" immigrants, not specifically "Jewish" immigrants, since he probably feared that too much ethnicity could limit the film's market appeal. (In "Yentl," director Barbra Streisand spared nothing as far as ethnic color is concerned and did very well at the box office!)

In one particular respect, however, "Avalon" is very effective—in its portrayal of the struggle of typical, hard-working immigrants in post WWII America. Here, two very ambitious young men, sons of Polish Jews (paperhangers), are doing

---

[16]Georgia Brown, The Village Voice, October 9, 1990. Terry Barr echoes the exact sentiments: "Though Avalon's characters are Jewish, their Jewishness never seems central for them; in fact, the depictions of family gatherings, the question of shortening and anglicizing Jewish names, and the bringing over of European Jewish family members are not shown as Jewish acts as much as they are personal ones to preserve the family as Americans and not necessarily as Jews"(in "Eating Kosher, Staying Closer," p. 137). Levinson redeems himself in "Liberty Heights" (1999), an autobiographical film on growing up Jewish in 1950s Baltimore. Unlike "Avalon," this work is replete with Yiddishisms, discussions of ethnicity, anti-Semitism and religion.

everything necessary to succeed in the "Promised Land." They sacrifice free time, family time, holidays, they economize. But, for our purposes, even most importantly, they change their names from the Polish-Jewish "Krichinsky" to the much more Waspish-sounding "Kaye" and "Kirk." We need to remember that these are the 1950s, which were prosperous times in America; ironically, like many other Jewish entrepreneurs, they too benefit from the war in Europe. While the "Kaye" and "Kirk" heads of households are well off financially, one wonders about their role as heads of presumably Jewish families. As presented here, practically nothing ethnic/religious is passed on, neither in the form of education, nor in shared traditions.

While it is true that immigrants wanted to blend in, they rarely chose the radical assimilation course presented by Levinson. I suspect that this director is simply dishonest, that his work's ethnic ambiguities are simply the product of unfounded fear of diminished market value should his product turn out to be "too Jewish."

"Lost in Yonkers" is another example of vapid ethnicity. This is one of Neil Simon's nostalgic recreations of childhood experiences in the early 1940s in and around New York. ("Brighton Beach Memoirs" is another.) "Lost in Yonkers" takes place almost entirely in Yonkers, then a quiet suburb of New York City. It is summer, 1942. Financial hardships force the recently widowed Eddie to deposit his teenage boys, Jay and Arty, at Grandma Kurnitz's in Yonkers while he goes off to the South in search of scrap metal to sell to companies making weapons and ammunition for the fighting army. Grandma (Irene Worth) is notorious for her bad temper, meanness and stinginess. She is a German Jew, owner of a corner candy store, a tough old lady with a cane, an immigrant who prides herself on not having cried in years. In fact, she has no tolerance for any displays of softness or sentimentality. In the words of one displeased critic, she is "a sadistic mother, a Jewish dictator who talks like Henry Kissinger."[17]

Her rotten disposition seems to originate in an accident that happened in her youth, in Berlin, during a Nazi rally when a horse went out of control and crushed her foot. More misery follows as she later loses a husband and child to various illnesses. These loses harden her even more: she foreswears to never again feel love towards anyone, thus protecting herself from ever getting hurt. The main recipients of this cynicism and bitterness are her children. Not surprisingly, they all grow up to become maladjusted adults. Bella (Mercedes Ruehl), a single, 36-year-old woman with a heart of gold but the emotional maturity of an adolescent, is one of her daughters. She still lives with grandma. Her sister Gert, lives in Yonkers too, but she avoids grandma like the plague. She is angry at her; she cannot forgive the physical and emotional abuse inflicted on her by the old woman who locked her up in a closet for hours at end, scaring her for life. Grandma's bachelor son, Louie, (Richard Dreyfus) is a small-time mobster in New York. He visits grandma only when chased by disgruntled competitors, or when he runs out of money.

Typically, the women in this largely dysfunctional immigrant family assume traditional roles of housekeepers. The males, on the other hand, work very hard pursuing the "American Dream." Eddie and Louie are ambitious men; while one chases the dream by traditional means—working as a middleman in the scrap-metal industry—the other hopes to achieve his goals by committing minor crimes. Despite their rather desperate situation (Eddie is broke and pressured by loan sharks; Louie owes money to mobsters), they never lose hope. Like most children of immigrants, they believe that in America anything is possible, that these are only temporary

---

[17] Georgia Brown, The Village Voice, October 9, 1990.

setbacks easily overcome by hard work and perseverance. No doubt, some of the strong work ethic is inherited since this German mother's credo is "work, work, work."

It is not clear whether the two sons will indeed recover and start off on the road to economic success. Coolidge, the film's director, leaves no doubt, however, that Aunt Bella's future is a promising one as we follow her gradual progression from submissive daughter to independent woman. In fact, in the film's final, and one of its moving scenes, Aunt Bella, valise in hand, is leaving Yonkers for independence and a new life in sunny Florida.

As in "Avalon," unless we pay a great deal of attention, we are bound to miss the fact that what we are watching is actually a Jewish family. The first hint occurs when Jay reminds Aunt Bella that his mother is dead and buried in Beth Israel cemetery in the Bronx. Later, Jay speaks of his father, roaming the South for scrap metal, as "some Jew in Alabama" in search of a treasure. Grandma, the first generation immigrant, however, is not overheard saying anything Jewish or, for that matter, anything in Yiddish. She does utter a few Germanisms like the occasional "Dummkopf" ("Stupid") or "Gott in Himmel" ("God in Heaven"). While it is true that most German Jews spoke German, not Yiddish, even the most assimilated German Jews had something Jewish in their home—a menorah, a mezuzzah—and would on occasion refer to a religious holiday, a Bar-Mitzvah or the like. Moreover, it is only reasonable to expect that any adult Jew living in America in the 1940s would show some concern about the fate of Europe's persecuted Jews. Yet, it is only the 15-year-old Jay who says anything even remotely related to these cataclysmic world events—how his father's scrap metal business is helping the war effort. Most amazing though is Coolidge's cemetery scene in Yonkers. First, the camera focuses on Aunt Bella by the family plot, then it briefly pans over other graves—not a

Hebrew letter, not one Star of David in sight!

These films represent two distinctly different cinematic approaches to the Jewish immigrant experience in America. Newcomers are shown struggling with the pains of adjusting to a new life in a new and radically different country than the country of origin. Without exception, immigrant stories deal in some way or another with the difficult balancing act of absorbing "new world" values while preserving some "old world" ones. Directors Joan Micklin Silver ("Hester Street," "Crossing Delancey"), Paul Mazursky ("Enemies, A Love Story"), Larry Peerce ("Goodbye, Columbus") and Ernest Lehman ("Portnoy's Complaint") have presented this process of integration by placing their characters and plots in an unambiguously ethnic context. Barry Levinson ("Avalon") and Martha Coolidge ("Lost in Yonkers"), on the other hand, marginalize Jewish ethnicity to the degree that their works become typical of all immigrant experience regardless of religion or country of origin. Both—the more ethnically Jewish works as well as the other, less Jewish ones—are fine depictions of the complexities of the early immigrant experience in America. No doubt, some film maker is hard at work trying to create screen images of the life of America's new immigrants from the former Soviet Union.

Liberty Heights

Barry Levinson, 1999. Director Barry Levinson returns to familiar territory with his latest Baltimore memoir. But, unlike "Avalon," "Liberty Heights" is rich with Jewish ethnic color. The Kurtzmans—grandmother, parents and the two sons Van and Ben—are oftentimes engaged in conversations about such Jewish things as their Gentile neighbors, religious holidays, Bar-Mitzvahs and anti-Semitism. Jews are shown praying in synagogue, the Bubbe speaks Yiddish, while Nate (Joe Mantegna) and Ada Kurtzman (Bebe Neuwirth) use a variety of yiddishisms and exhibit typical ethnic mannerisms.

While the film is aglow with 1950s nostalgia, it is by no means another sentimental look at the life and times of America's post-war generation. For one, Levinson's Nate Kurtzman is a far cry from the stereotypical Jewish husband-type seen in so many movies of this period. While Nate is indeed the great Jewish male provider, his work is anything but eliciting of our admiration: he is running a burlesque establishment and a numbers operation on the side. Ironically, Nate seems to be oblivious of the hypocrisy of, on the one hand, being involved in highly immoral and illegal acts and, on the other, exhorting his two sons to be "good Jews," especially in their choice of female companions. As fate would have it, one son is infatuated with Dubbie, the fantasy *shiksa* girl (played by supermodel Carolyn Murphy), Levinson's version of Sybil Shepherd, that quintessential Wasp princess who breaks every young man's heart in the "The Last Picture Show," a 1950s work as well. The other son is in love with Sylvia, the only black girl in his highschool class. A great deal of the film's time is taken up with these two young men's struggles to maintain some form of relationships with the "forbidden fruits" of their strong desire.

While set in a distinctly Jewish context, Levinson's "Liberty Heights" dramatizes the Jewish desire to assimilate, the wish to break out of traditional ties and religious constraints. In some ways Nate's sons bring to mind Philip Roth's famous *shiksa*-obsessed Alex Portnoy; the difference is that these Baltimore boys are basically two very healthy young men irresistibly drawn to something they cannot or should not have, much like today's youth is attracted to experimenting with dangerous drugs.

The Longest Hatred: Hollywood Confronts Anti-Semitism

In the pivotal scene of Edward Dmytryk's "Crossfire" (1947), a drunken sergeant named Montgomery (Robert Ryan) becomes enraged at a stranger named Joseph Samuels and kills him. Like Macbeth's noble Malcolm, a Detective named Finley (Robert Young) arrives at the bar in Washington, DC, where the murder has taken place—a messenger of goodness amidst hatred—and restores order.

Later, during the film's denouement, Finley lectures a group of policemen about the dangers of prejudice. He describes the experience of Irish immigrants who came to America a century earlier because of the deadly famine in their country. Instead of tolerance and goodwill, many of the fleeing Irishmen found bigotry and violence in their adopted country. All they heard was that they were drunkards, priest lovers, spies for the Pope, and a whole array of other offensive epithets. Some were beaten; others, like his grandfather, were murdered in the streets. "Last night," says Finley, "Joseph Samuels was killed because he was a Jew. It could strike anyone."

Today it's hard to take the film seriously. Finley condemns the murder not just because of its anti-Semitic motivation, but because it demonstrates that no one is safe from prejudice. Yet at no point does John Paxtone's script—set in Washington, DC no less—make any reference to prejudice against blacks. Even viewers in the late 1940s, less sensitive than modern audiences to the vagaries of racism, noticed this conspicuous omission. How can a fable about Middle American prejudice fail to address the plight of its oppressed black population? James Agee of The Nation, one among many critics who praised the film, pointed out that its producers lacked the courage to address the potentially loaded topic of race relations.[1]

The makers of "Crossfire" do make sure Montgomery utters almost every anti-Semitic slur known in the English language. A native of the rural south, he calls

---

[1] James Agee, The Nation (August 2, 1947).

Samuels a "New York type" of "Jewboy," and, who, according to Montgomery, enjoyed the good life of rich city Jews with funny sounding names, all this while workers and farmers risked their lives to fight Hitler in Europe. He claimed he knew the type well: most of them got out of army service and those who did serve secured themselves cushy jobs. Montgomery also claims to know that they are, without exception, cunning, cowardly and weak.

Montgomery represents the primitive anti-Semite, one who requires neither religious dogma nor nationalistic fervor. Walter Sokel has called such personalities "ontological anti-Semites," bigots who hate Jews "simply for existing."[2] The sergeant's paranoid and obsessive persona is plagued with self-doubt, cowardice, greed and immaturity (a plum role for an over-the-top actor like Ryan who might have won the Oscar too had Edmund Gwenn not been so perfect as another stock gentile in "Miracle on 34th Street"). With his undefined hatred of the "other," it remains all the more bizarre that the film never shows him in confrontation with any other minority group.

A different type of anti-Semitism preoccupies Elia Kazan in "Gentleman's Agreement" (1947)—one that is more refined. The unspoken snub of the corporate board room or of the posh country club, Gregory Peck plays Phil Green, a journalist called by a leading liberal New York publication to write an investigative piece on anti-Semitism in America. Green, the method journalist, decides to pose as a Jew. The ruse works. He gets a terrific scoop, as he is summarily shut out of social

---

[2] Walter Sokel, "Dualistic Thinking and the Rise of Ontological Antisemitism in Nineteenth Century Germany: From Schiller's Franz Moor to Wilhelm Raabe's Moses Freudenstein," in Sander Gilman and Steven Katz, eds. Antisemitism in Times of Crisis (New York: New York University Press, 1991), p. 154. On anti-Semitism in America see: Arthur Hertzberg, The Jews in America (New York: Simon & Schuster, 1989) and Leonard Dinnerstein, Antisemitism in America (New York: Oxford University Press, 1988).

circles, cheated through a clause in his apartment lease, and unable to book a room in a prestigious, WASPS-only hotel. His doctor warns him to avoid a certain physician with a "German" last name. His well-bred girlfriend (Dorothy McGuire) almost leaves him when her bigoted family and friends from the Connecticut suburbs start to make unsavory comments. His son is called a "kike" and "dirty Jew" by his classmates who mistake him for a Jew.

This high culture anti-Semitism remains more slippery and difficult to combat. To avoid legal entanglements, organizations invent creative ways to exclude undesirables. Public figures avoid making explicitly disparaging remarks. Green has trouble substantiating the anit-Semitism he encounters. Though never explored in the film, one suspects that his final expose may have been applauded publicly and then promptly forgotten as social norms of prejudice resumed their natural course. These norms were so deeply ingrained, Jews themselves were generally leery of challenging them. A recent New York Times article describes how producer Darryl F. Zanuck's Jewish colleagues in the film industry tried to dissuade him from the project altogether: "For Chrissake, why make that picture? We're getting along all right. Why raise the whole subject?" Zanuck told them to "mind their own business," that "it was the right time."[3] Twenty years earlier, another Zanuck movie, "The Jazz Singer" had broached a social issue (racial discrimination) in the same hesitant matter.

Several critics, like The New Yorker's John McCarten, wondered if the film's serious theme had been buried under its subplots and glamour, including the story of controversial core. His criticism of the book's author, Laura Hobson, is especially

---

[3]These comments are found in: George F. Custen, "Over 50 Years, A Landmark Loses Some of its Luster," The New York Times (November 16, 1997).

biting: "It is her conviction that anti-Semitism can be defeated by renting Jews houses in 'restrictive' areas and by not listening to dull jokes."[4] Just as "Crossfire" avoids the more explosive discussion of prejudice against blacks, so does "Gentleman's Agreement" remain a bit too gentlemanly to raise eyebrows higher than absolutely necessary.

Hollywood's liberal conscience, it seemed, could evoke tasteful tears and self-righteous applause, but not if that meant threatening the status quo. These films were made by many of the industry's iconoclastic young guard. The older moguls —Zanuck excepted, and he wasn't even Jewish—were far too cautious to advance Jewish causes through their pictures. In the two decades preceding the full knowledge of the Holocaust, American film makers were trying to maneuver amid charges of Jews as instigators of the war in Europe, Jews as financiers of war machines, and Jews as profiteers.[5] Judging purely by what was on screen in those days, one would have thought that Hollywood was dominated by one religious group—Irish priests. Perhaps in the end the older moguls were right to fear a backlash, for soon, in the early 1950s, the "House Committee on Un-American Activities," fueled in part by a barely hidden anti-Semitism, would begin its anti-Communist witch hunt in Hollywood. Many of the progressive figures involved in these films, including Kazan and Dmytryk, found themselves forced to testify or go

---

[4] John McCarten, The New Yorker (November 15, 1947).

[5] Lester D. Friedman, Hollywood's Image of the Jew (New York: Frederick Ungar Publishing Co., 1982), Chapter 3: "The Fashionable Forties."

to jail.[6]

Ironically, both pictures lack a central feature one might have expected in major films about anti-Semitism: Jews. They may debate at length how Jews must feel in an anti-Semitic environment, but the victims themselves barely make the supporting cast. As Lester Friedman correctly observes, "both 'Crossfire' and 'Gentleman's Agreement' do little more than skirt the issue of American antisemitism."[7]

Thus, in "Crossfire," Samuels appears for a few minutes before he is murdered. The audience never learns how he felt as a Jewish G.I. in Japan, how he coped in a predominantly Christian and probably hostile environment. The two Jews in "Gentleman's Agreement"—Green's childhood friend David and his secretary—are thoroughly assimilated. Green's secretary has even changed her name, lest anyone suspect her true identity. When someone suggests that the company hire Jews, she expresses concern that "they'll be of the wrong kind," that, God forbid, they will not try to hide their identity, that they might even flaunt it. The picture itself studiously avoids dealing with any aspect of Judaism, Jewish culture or Jewishly-committed Jews. Did the film makers perceive the self-reflexive parody of their own final product? Were they, also, afraid their movie might seem too Jewish?

These questions must have remained sensitive for a long time, because it took Hollywood 45 years to return to this controversial topic in its popular films.

---

[6]The controversy over McCarthyism and Jewish intellectuals resurfaced recently in Hollywood's decision to bestow the "Lifetime Achievement Award" on Elia Kazan who divulged names of colleagues to the now infamous Congressional committee investigating what it termed as "subversive, communist activities" by prominent Americans in the entertainment industry. In fact, "Names" is the title of a recent play by Mark Kemble about some of those persecuted figures—the legendary "Group Theater" and its Jewish members: Clifford Odets, John Garfield, Lee Strassberg, Stella Adler and Harold Clurman.

[7]Lester Friedman, p. 128.

Although the respective social contexts of Robert Mandel's "School Ties" (1992) and Robert Redford's "Quiz Show" (1993) are vastly different from the earlier films and from one another, both works retain their earlier models' cautiously pareve (lukewarm) approach to anti-Semitism. With all of their sanitized understatements, the exclusive New England boarding school depicted in "School Ties" and the television production room in "Quiz Show" could have been easily confused with the fancy hotel that sent Gregory Peck packing.

Unlike the sophisticated, marginal Jews of the earlier films, the hero of "School Ties" is the son (Brendan Fraser) of Jewish blue-collar workers from Scranton, Pennsylvania. David Greene is a gifted football player who receives an athletic scholarship to a private prep school.[8] While his stuffy non-Jewish peers admire David's performance in class and on the football field, school officials do all in their power to conceal his religious identity. When he arrives on campus, the football coach advises him not to make a fuss about any "particular eating habits." The student himself removes his Star of David from his neck, sings at the Sunday morning church service, and participates in benedictions in the cafeteria. He even plays ball on Rosh Hashana. After the game, when everyone else is asleep, he guiltily sneaks to the chapel to pray. The Headmaster overhears his recital of Avinu Malkenu and sternly rebukes him.

Eager to please, David is careful not to react to the occasional anti-Semitic remark. When a history teacher discovers that someone has cheated on the test, the culprit—one of the most bigoted students on campus—implicates David: "Who else

---

[8]One could compare the experiences of this Jewish athlete with those of H. M. Abrahams, a world-class runner at Oxford who competed for England in the 1924 Olympics. Abrahams is the main character of "Chariots of Fire" (1978), a film directed by Hugh Hudson and produced by Dody Fayed, Princess Diana's lover and one of the victims of the September 1997 fatal car crash in Paris.

but a Jew would dishonor the code?" With no allies and sensing the futility of denial, David accepts the blame. Someone paints a swastika on his dorm wall. He challenges the anonymous vandal to a fight, but no one steps forward. Against the stereotypes, David proves to be an excellent athlete and a student with integrity, and finally he is exonerated. The film ends with the hope that perhaps, he, too, will be admitted to the Ivy League of his and his classmate's dreams.

In "Gentleman's Agreement" a gentile plays a Jew and pays a price for his calculated risk; in "School Ties," a Jew acts like a gentile and is rewarded for his conformity. While the progressive 1990s film makers can be bold enough to feature a Jewish main character, his personal redemption comes only through complete acculturation. We note screenwriter Ring Lardner's remarks about the 1947 film: "The film's lesson? You should never be mean to a Jew because he might turn out to be a gentile."[9] Both films show that anti-Semitism is ultimately a non-Jewish problem. If only gentiles would realize that Jews are the same in every respect, we could all live together, intermarry, and become one big indistinguishable family, Hollywood style.

The producers of "School Ties" explained to The New York Times that they were motivated to make the movie because of discrimination they themselves suffered. Thus, the late Sherry Lansing, once president of "20th Century Fox," recalled being told by another mother that a certain school in the Hamptons was not acceptable because "they had too many Jews there."[10] The late Brandon Tartikoff, former chairman of "Paramount," remembers bullies hurling anti-Semitic remarks

---

[9]Lardner's comments are found in Custen's article (see footnote #3).

[10]Bernard Weinraub, "An Antisemitism Film that Strikes a Chord," The New York Times (September 14, 1992).

at him in a Long Island private school in the 1950s.[11] Stanley Jaffe, president of "Paramount Communications," learned that even in the early 1980s a number of his friends could not live in certain exclusive Manhattan buildings because they were Jews.[12] These incidents may have been upsetting, but they make a weaker-than-dishwasher premise for a story on a weighty theme like anti-Semitism. By the time David finds the offending swastika on his door, one already suspects Laura Hobson was somehow involved with the original screenplay.

In "Quiz Show," the character of Herb Stempel (John Turturro) is that welcome rarity in films about anti-Semitism: an unembarrassed Jew from Queens who not only looks Jewish, but lives in a Jewish neighborhood and boasts Jewish friends. He's even married to a Jew! And she bakes delicious rugelach to boot! Robert Redford's film looks behind the scenes of "Twenty One," a popular 1950s game show that happens to be fixed. Despite Stempel's phenomenal memory and intelligence, the producers secretly supply him with all of the questions and answers in advance. Stempel, it turns out, is supposed to win for only so long, until a new hero named Charles Van Doren (Ralph Fiennes) is found to replace him. Handsome and pedigreed, Van Doren the Columbia professor, holds greater promise for the show's ratings as the new star contestant. Stempel appears unkempt, sweaty and ethnic. Van Doren is elegant, blond and blue eyed.

After being coached to miss a question intentionally, Stempel becomes furious. In a loud confrontation, he accuses the producer of ousting him for being Jewish. The producer denied it, then privately derides Stempel's background and appearance. Just as the film starts to suggest the anti-Semitic underpinnings of the

---

[11] Ibid.

[12] Ibid.

television world, it turns abruptly to a totally different moral theme—dishonesty in the media. Not only does this sudden transition seem uneven aesthetically, it makes the viewer wonder if the film makers became afraid of the discriminatory angle—perhaps a little too close to home for comfort?—and sought refuge under a more tepid formula. The remainder of the story deals with the Justice Department's investigation of game shows as an industry. Once again, on the verge of confronting the darker social implications of anti-Semitism, film maker's retreat to a one-dimensional theme that guarantees a crisper, more satisfying climax.

What's most striking is that in an interview in The New Yorker, the real Stempel had said nothing about Jewishness being a factor in his dismissal.[13] He was bitter because he felt betrayed. NBC had simply made the more popular choice of contestants, especially for its women viewers. Why then bring up Stempel's Jewishness at all on screen? The anti-Semitism leitmotif, brief in its appearance, seems to have been introduced only as a dependable contrivance, just as Gregory Peck's girl gets cold feet and Brendan Fraser is forced to say grace. Hollywood's rendition of anti-Semitism seems to have graduated into its own mini-genre: the minor bourgeois annoyances of social discrimination. Leave the stinging, controversial and dangerous sides of hatred of Jews to the scholars and the ADL.

Perhaps it is unfair to expect so much from a medium so unabashedly borne of breadwinning. Why would any self-respecting Hollywood producer or director take on a theme that is, by its jarring nature, going to turn away audiences? Better audiences should go home feeling reassured, inspired by Robert Young's rousing lecture, relieved that Peck gets his girl, hopeful of Fraser's Ivy League placement, and content that Stempel at least profits enough from the game show to supply his

---

[13]Review of "Quiz Show" in The New Yorker (June 21, 1993).

rugelach fix indefinitely. In this feel-good industry, anti-Semitism exists only to provide temporary dramatic tension, not to challenge viewers to reexamine the more menacing forces of their society.

Black Hats on the Silver Screen: Religious Life in America

A talis and tefillin craze in Hollywood? Not exactly. But sometimes fiction is stranger than truth. In recent decades the movie industry has generally been kind to so-called "black hats," sometimes even creating romantic images of their lifestyle.[1]

Compared with Woody Allen's satire of religious Jews in early comedies like "Take the Money and Run" (1969), and "Bananas" (1971), and his more scathing recent depiction of them in "Deconstructing Harry," other modern works have radically changed the way traditional Judaism is shown on screen. In Jeremy Kagan's "The Chosen" (1982), Barbra Streisand's "Yentl" (1983), Sidney Lumet's "A Stranger Among Us" (1992) and Boaz Yakin's "A Price Above Rubies" (1998), bearded Jews are no longer comical and marginal figures, but three-dimensional characters who command the audience's attention and, occasionally, even its sympathy.

Chaim Potok's classic 1967 novel, The Chosen, is a rich and complex work, probably inspired by the impending Arab-Israeli war and the Civil Rights movement sweeping America at the time of its publication. The book features elaborate debates between pro-Zionist and anti-Zionist Jews, and their preoccupation with the importance of tolerance and understanding within the fractured, feuding Jewish community. The novel's multidimensional view of Brooklyn in the 1930s and 1940s becomes, in Kagan's cinematic interpretation, another tale of hard-nosed rebels

---

[1] The interest in religious Jews is not limited to films; several popular novels, including Alegra Goodman's Kaaterskill Falls, Tova Reich's The Jewish War, and Pearl Abraham's Giving Up America, depict issues confronting observant or Hasidic groups in America today. The Jewish print media has begun to take notice of this phenomenon. Among others, it points out that in recent years religion has increasingly moved from the private to the public sphere, that mainstream culture is much more accepting of Orthodoxy, even Hasidism, than it had only a generation ago. See: Peter Ephross, "Observant American Jews Portrayed in Novels and on Film," Jewish Standard (November 20, 1998); Aviva Kempner, "Finally, Jewish Women Have Sex on the Screen," Lilith (Spring, 1999).

defying dominant social norms and expectations.

The story's heroes are Danny Saunders (Robby Benson) and Reuven Malter (Barry Miller). They meet on a baseball field, each playing for a different team. During the game, Danny inadvertently pitches a ball at Reuven's face, injuring his eye. During Reuven's stay in the hospital and his recuperation at home, the two become close friends. Their relationship does not seem unusual. But Danny is the son of the famous Reb Saunders (Rod Steiger), leader of an Hasidic sect in Brooklyn. Reuven is the son of a secular Talmudist, Dr. Malter (Maximilian Schell), Reb Saunders' spiritual and intellectual adversary.

Although he is expected to follow his father's path as the next Rebbe, Danny secretly reads Freud and other prohibited books. Instead of devoting himself to a lifetime of religious studies and leadership, Danny decides to study at the university. Reuven, who is never pressured by his father about career choices, follows the scholar's footsteps.[2] He will further his Talmudic studies and become a rabbi— naturally, an enlightened and modern rabbi. The film presents both young men as determined, tough-minded, all-American boys, about to embark on separate but equally promising careers. Their trials and tribulations, though set in a Jewish environment, become universal by the end of the film. Mutatis mutandis, they could have been two Irish boys facing similar problems as sons of first generation Americans in New York. Still, the unimposing Jewish background remains quaint and appealing throughout the drama.

---

[2] Robert Hatch of The Nation (May 8, 1982) finds the Rebbe's behavior incredulous, that an autocrat "who until then had flown into a passion over any hint of resistance to his divinely sanctioned wisdom would abruptly turn benign and release his heir from his destined role in life. Nor do I believe that arbitrary and unprovoked punishment would produce the superlative young man Danny is shown to be." Judith Crist of The Saturday Review (April, 1982), on the other hand, was impressed by Kagan's handling of the main characters, especially the Rebbe's son, and of the relationship between the two young men.

Though set in 1904, "somewhere in Eastern Europe," "Yentl" is remarkably similar to Streisand's earlier Americana movies, "Funny Girl" and "Hello Dolly." In all three Streisand is talented, strong willed and independent. All of her characters achieve their goals by defying stereotypes and by breaking patriarchal structures.

In Yentl's case society dictates that she limit herself to household chores while waiting patiently to assume the role of a "proper" Jewish wife and mother. But Yentl, based on a character in an Isaac Bashevis Singer story, is not like all Jewish girls in her village. Secretly, and with her father's assistance, she studies the Bible and the Talmud. When he dies, she dresses as a boy named Anchel and attempts to conquer the male world of the yeshiva.[3]

Complications arise when she falls in love with her study partner, Avigdor. Avigdor is engaged to Hadas, the daughter of a wealthy Jew in town. When the wealthy father suddenly calls off the wedding after learning about mental illness in Avigdor's family, Yentl/Anchel replaces the groom. In what seems a time warp fresh from the 1980s, the new groom sets out to make the docile Hadas into a modern and independent woman. Yentl introduces her to the concepts of gender-role rebellion and resistance to tradition, and they all live liberated ever after. The domain of the yeshiva suits Streisand just fine as an antiquated foil; all in all, Streisand's Jewish world of the past emerges as a cozy and idyllic place.

"A Stranger Among Us" is set in present-day Hasidic Brooklyn. The formulaic plot revolves around a mysterious crime committed inside the close-knit

---

[3]David Danby, in a review entitled, "Educating Barbra," is not sure he knows why "Yentl" had to educate herself: "We never get much idea of what all this learning is for. Is the Talmud really worth knowing? Or is studying it just a boy's game of matching wits that Streisand admires because the game is closed to girls?" (New York Magazine, November 28, 1983). Pauline Kael, on the other hand, views "Yentl" as the product of a sensitive, feminine hand, at times, even a feminist one. (The New Yorker, November 28, 1983).

Jewish community. The attractive Emily Eden (Melanie Griffith) is a successful detective, but unsuccessful in her love life. She wants desperately to meet her true love when—as fate and the scriptwriters would have it—her work brings her to Brooklyn and to him, to Ariel, another heir apparent to an Hasidic dynasty. Of course, though worlds apart, they quickly become friends, like most blond Presbyterians and zealous religious prodigies would, under the same circumstances. With great self-discipline, they prevent the romance they recognize would be devastating for both of them, as well as for the film's already wildly improbable screenplay.

During the investigation of the murder, Emily learns a great deal about Hasidic Judaism, including the mystical teachings of the Kabbala. Ariel and others tell her about the concept of bashert, how people are matched mystically with their true love at birth. When asked how exactly to identify one's bashert, Ariel enigmatically responds: "You will know." Armed with this new wisdom, Emily comes away more confident than ever. In the final scene, after the murder is solved and Ariel is married to his own, clearly non-Presbyterian bashert, Emily's only Jewish partner on the police force invites her to spend a weekend in the Bahamas. She might have considered the offer at another time in her life, but she now prefers to wait for the "Right Guy."

"A Price Above Rubies" is also set in present-day Hasidic Brooklyn. The protagonist is Sonia Horowitz (Renee Zellweger), a young Orthodox woman. Freshly married and with a baby, Sonia realizes that her life in this monolithic Borough Park Hasidic community is going to be that of most women there: devoted wife and mother, basically playing the role of supporting cast to husbands who worry about finances or, as in her case, a husband obsessed with religious studies and worshiping at the feet of his Rebbe. Dissatisfied with these prospects, Sonia decides to work for her brother-in-law, a successful jeweler. On her way to realizing her potential, she gradually severs her ties to the religious community and her family. In the end, she and her husband Mendl get a divorce. Apprehensive but hopeful, Sonia leaves everything behind, including her baby, and sets off to start a new life. As Maria Garcia notes, "A Price Above Rubies" is "about the price we pay for consciousness and for self-realization."[4]

Although most of these films are unusually kind to their subjects, the Jews depicted therein probably would never visit movie theaters themselves. The Hasidim in "The Chosen" appear in the streets, in synagogue, inside the Rebbe's home. They revere their Rebbe and are fiercely loyal to him and his family. They mistrust the outside world and are uneasy whenever Danny appears in public with the secular Reuven. They dedicate themselves to self-sacrifice and self-control, and seem perennially engaged in serious Talmudic disputations—it's almost a shame most real yeshiva students won't learn from their idealized cinematic counterparts.

The Rebbe, as played by Steiger, is an awe-inspiring religious figure. All obey his wishes, except his own son. His larger-than-life tragic presence, as critic Judith Crist described in <u>The Saturday Review</u>, is "all aglow with Rembrandtesque lighting."[5] Sparing his words like precious jewels, his tragedy is compounded by the fact that he is a Holocaust survivor whose children from a previous marriage were lost in concentration camps. Danny is his only hope of preserving the dynasty.

Kagan makes all the ecstatic shuckling in prayer, lively celebrations and joy of life believably compelling, diminished only by Steiger's muddy Hebrew and Yiddish accents and other minor inaccuracies. Danny says Baruch Hashem with

---

[4] Maria Garcia, "A Price Above Rubies," <u>Film Journal International</u> (March, 1998), p. 122.

[5] Judith Crist, <u>The Saturday Review</u> (April, 1982).

modern Hebrew pronunciation instead of the Boruch or Bureech that characterize his era. The viewer wonders why Reuven's father, the secular American scholar, is portrayed by a German actor.

Streisand must have learned from Kagan's mistakes, eliminating accents altogether. Except for occasional toasts of *l'chaim* or *mazel tov*, Hebrew and Yiddish are strangely absent in her simulated world. Her yeshiva *bochers* speak articulate, unaccented English.

Unlike the seriousness of the Brooklyn Jews, Streisand's cast includes robust, cheery, youthful men—like students in a bucolic boarding school. David Danby in New York Magazine wondered whether there ever was a movie with so rhapsodic an attitude toward book learning "... scene after scene of young blackbeards excitedly expounding and disputing, their heads nodding, fingers waving in the air ... where the yeshiva is the center of the town activity ... where young women are anxious to marry these sober-suited champions, and bear their children...."[6]

Kagan's Hasidim seek spirituality in teachings, wisdom or the mere presence of their *tzaddik*, Reb Saunders. In "Yentl" the students go directly to the sources for spirituality, sometimes to train for careers in religious life, but sometimes for the transcendence of learning for its own sake. There is no personality cult here. Not that deep respect is absent, it is simply redirected toward God and those who master His Torah and Talmud. Avigdor is one of the more accomplished students, the *ilui*, who argues persuasively and remembers whole passages of text. These men have freer spirits and are closer to nature. They do not play baseball, they stay in shape by swimming au naturel in the river.

East-European yeshivas were never quite so romantic. Students lived in

---

[6]David Danby, New York Magazine (November 28, 1983).

cramped spaces, did not sport such healthy complexions, and suffered at the hands of ubiquitous anti-Semites. Violent pogroms would certainly have spoiled Streisand's aggressively lovely tone. Many critics who praised Streisand as an actor and director noticed the difference between the film's false nostalgic glow and the more sober Singer story that served as its basis.[7]

Like Kagan, Sidney Lumet introduces the figure of the mysterious Rebbe, Ariel's father. As leader of an Hasidic sect, he too is treated by his disciples with reverence and total obedience. But unlike Danny Saunders, Ariel does accept the yoke of tradition. Danny leaves the fold because he thirsts for secular knowledge. Working in the New York diamond district, Ariel has greater access to the outside world than Danny, but he seems content with his seemingly restrictive lifestyle.

Mendl, Sonia's husband in "A Price Above Rubies," is also devoted to learning and to his Rebbe. Like Ariel, he is committed to a fervently religious life, even at the price of losing his wife in the process. All Mendl needed to save his family was a little bit of compromising and attention to Sonia's needs. Fanaticism, as we all know, knows no compromise. Although the Rebbe does not appear in this film, his power over his followers is absolute. Mendl would do anything the Rebbe says he should do. In fact, he would not undertake anything new in his life without the leader's consent or advice. Unlike Danny Saunders, Mendl is totally uninterested in the outside world, in the pleasures and wonders of the free, secular world.

For Ariel, it is not forbidden knowledge that is the problem, but "forbidden fruit" in the form of Emily. The writers might have given the unfortunate detective a subtler last name than "Eden." Ariel views worldly knowledge and physical

---

[7]Pauline Kael, for one, compares the book and the film and draws similar conclusions. (The New Yorker, November 28, 1983).

pleasures as temptations to be overcome. He struggles like most decent human beings to live a higher spiritual existence despite his physical failings. His character is thoughtful and fully drawn. His presence alone dispels the perception of religious men and women as automatons, fanatics, devoid of human feelings and inner conflicts.

Like Streisand, Lumet surrounds his Brooklyn Jews with such a powerful glow of warmth that Yael Hadia in the Israeli daily, <u>Maariv</u>, suggested that while Lumet was on lunch break "some Lubavitcher Chassid must have crept up to the set to give explicit instructions to the crew."[8] "A Stranger Among Us" does offer a detailed, nuanced view of the Rebbe's home. Women work hard in the kitchen, various disciples and family members come and go, the leader assumes his extremely busy daily responsibilities. Harmony reigns. No one seems the worse for the lack of television sets, movies or theater. In addition to Kabbala lessons, Emily learns about traditional Jewish food, rules of modesty in dress and speech, rituals of courtship and matrimony, and mourning customs. What emerges is a picture of a close-knit community, a caring and generous group of people. Not surprisingly, the murderer turns out to be a stranger from the outside.

With few exceptions, the Hasidic world of "A Price Above Rubies" is, by contrast, depicted as a hypocritical, corrupt place. Sonia's brother-in-law (a married man with children) is having affairs at his "work studio" in Manhattan, with Sonia as one of the women he seduces. As soon as Sonia shows signs of non-conformity, the women in Mendl's family conspire to rob her of her baby, arguing that she is a "bad mother" for doing so. Family values, as practiced by these Orthodox women,

---

[8]Yael Hadia, "Melanie Griffith ochelet tzimes umitaheved bebachur yeshiva." ("Melanie Griffith eats tzimes and falls in love with a Yeshiva student.") <u>Maariv</u> (Israeli daily newspaper, August 14, 1992).

have just assumed a totally new meaning!

Judging by the long-running popularity of these films, the choice of ultra-orthodox settings for these stories of general human interest seems to have been wise. This is not the first time Hollywood gambled with exotic religious groups. "A Stranger Among Us" borrows unapologetically from Peter Weir's "Witness" (1985), in which crime unsettles the Amish community. Ultimately stars and plot suspense draw audiences to movies. But the unusual settings add to the appeal. "A Price Above Rubies" notwithstanding, the public seems drawn towards these characters' stubborn resistance to the fast-paced and chaotic modern world. Subconsciously, they admire and maybe even envy the strong beliefs, moral values and communal adhesiveness. Drawn into the idyllic, audiences can more easily conceive of their own world in all of its potential as a simpler, safer and more wholesome place to live.

Spinoza Confronts the Rabbis: An Israeli Film and Play

Three hundred years after his death, Spinoza continues to fascinate. In this decade alone, the controversial seventeenth-century philosopher has been revived on stage by Joshua Sobol in "Solo Lespinoza" (1991) and on the screen by Igal Bursztyn in "Everlasting Joy—The Life and Adventures of Baruch Spinoza" (1996).[1] Typically, the play and the film draw from both myth and historical sources. Before touching on these two artistic works, it is necessary to understand his basic philosophy, the circumstances leading to his excommunication, and the image of this world-renowned Jewish intellectual in popular Israeli and Jewish culture.

Spinoza comes down through history as the champion of such treasured liberal notions as individual freedoms and rights, the separation of Church and State, and independence from any kind of dominant or established religious authority or dogma. He is viewed as the archetypical intellectual revolutionary, a scholar who had the courage to stand by his ideas and fight the mighty forces of the religious and political establishment. Also, he is seen as one who broke with accepted norms of thinking, and broke with deeply-rooted traditions. He was a man of principle who successfully resisted the seductive powers of wealth and social status. In short, he is an admired martyr figure who accepted suffering rather than compromise his strongly held views. Invariably, his actions have served as a paradigm for both religious and political discourse.

In broad terms Spinoza espoused a pantheistic view of the universe whereby God is nature itself and not some omnipotent deity that at one point created the world, performed miracles, and gave humanity laws and rules. In Jewish terms, this meant that the Torah (the written law) and the Rabbinic tradition (the oral law) were

---

[1] Joshua Sobol, <u>Solo LeSpinoza</u> (Tel Aviv: Or Am, 1991). My translation of the play is unpublished. A recent book on him is: <u>Steven Smith, Spinoza, Liberalism, and the Question of Jewish Identity</u> (New Haven: Yale University Press, 1997).

not Divinely inspired and therefore, not binding. In the words of preeminent Spinoza scholar, Yermiyahu Yovel, for Spinoza, Biblical ordinances and halachic rules "seemed arbitrary and merely historical, having nothing to do with the laws of God. If God did indeed have laws, they could only be inherent in the universe itself, in the form of the universal and immutable laws of nature."[2]

In effect Spinoza argued that, while worthy of admiration and serious study, the Commandments, the miracles in the desert, the prophesies, and volumes of rabbinic exegesis and writings are not to be revered as uncontroversial Divine revelations, but as imperfect products of human imagination and creativity.

As Yovel and others point out, Spinoza's heretical views might have been tolerated by the relatively liberal Jewish authorities had not the State itself (the Dutch authorities) felt threatened by them. This was a time of great upheaval as thousands of Jews were fleeing the Inquisition in Spain and Portugal for the more tolerant Holland, a place where they were allowed to practice their religion and traditions in relative freedom.

The doors of most Western European countries, most notably England, were closed to these Jews. The Dutch government knew this well. Though it did open its borders to these persecuted refugees, it nonetheless expected nothing less than exemplary civic behavior from them. As these Dutch leaders saw it, Spinoza's public statements and writings threatened to undermine much cherished Judeo-Christian beliefs, and basic moral foundations.

To opponents of Jewish immigration (various anti-Semitic groups), they amounted to treason at a time when the country had to stay united against dangerous enemies in France, England and elsewhere. Enemies of Jewish immigration in the

---

[2]Yirmiyahu Yovel, Spinoza and Other Heretics (Princeton: Princeton University Press, 1989), p. 4.

Dutch Parliament were trying to block them from entering on economic and political grounds, with Spinoza serving as their lightning rod. The same legislators used the "Spinoza affair" to argue against granting Marranos full citizenship under the law. In short, though immeasurably better off than in the Iberian Peninsula, Jews were in no position to irritate, provoke or alienate their hosts in the Netherlands. Faced with mounting pressures from within and without, the rabbis and *parnasim* (community leaders) of Amsterdam had no choice but to declare a *cherem* on him, i.e., to excommunicate Spinoza from the Jewish community.

This, then, is the background against which Sobol's play "Solo for Spinoza" is set. In comparing history and its artistic representation, the first thing that stands out is Sobol's elevation of Spinoza to tragic heights. According to Spinoza biographer R. H. M. Elwes, the philosopher was:

> very frugal in his way of living . . . he knew how to master his passions . . . was courteous and obliging . . . his amusements were very simple; talking on ordinary matters with the people of the house, smoking now and again a pipe of tobacco, watching the habits and quarrels of insects . . . absorbed in his work, sometimes for days at length . . . suffering from phthisis, a malady from which he died in 1677.[3]

Spinoza was rather frail, withdrawn and sickly, a loner who never married or had children. We also learn from Elwes that Spinoza lived largely on his inheritance, refusing financial assistance or job offers from the community or from universities, including the prestigious Heidelberg University in Germany.

Excommunication for the real Spinoza was, therefore, not such a terrible

---

[3] Benedict De Spinoza: A Theologico-Political Treatise and a Political Treatise, R. H. M. Elves, trans., and "Introduction" (New York: Dover Publications Inc., 1951). "Introduction," p. xix.

thing. To create a tragic effect, Sobol had to modify his character in such a way that banishment and social alienation would somehow mean a great deal. The Israeli dramatist created a hero resembling Brecht's reworking of Galileo, the famous Italian scientist and martyr figure, whose own heretical views placed him squarely opposite the Vatican.[4] Thus, Sobol's hero is a young man full of *"joie de vivre,"* a man obsessed with a prostitute, a heavy drinker, and a gourmand. By opposing the establishment and putting himself at grave risk, the historical Spinoza had to renounce few of life's pleasures; Sobol's Spinoza, on the other hand, has to give up a great deal that was dear to him for resisting authority. As Eugene Falk correctly points out, martyrdom is not really tragic when

> the martyr is impervious to his suffering because, as he perceives it, his cause exceeds the value of life. In such instances, though he does sacrifice his life, he does not renounce its joys, for he regards them with indifference, perhaps even with contempt. Consequently, tragic martyrdom occurs only when the higher value of the martyr's cause and the somewhat lower value of a renounced life are given serious consideration.[5]

Sobol, like Brecht, recognized that to heighten the tragic image of their martyr-like heroes—both highly controversial, anti-Church, anti-establishment figures—they had to be cast as life-loving creatures, not as fanatic crusaders for their

---

[4] Bertolt Brecht, Leben des Galilei (Frankfurt: Suhrkamp Verlag, 1973). English version: Galileo, Charles Laughton trans. (New York: Grove Press, 1966). Brecht wrote Galileo while in exile in 1938-39. For Brecht, who was watching Germany March in step with the Nazis, Galileo's act of defiance must have been inspirational. Unlike Spinoza, who submitted to banishment rather than compromise, Galileo struck a deal with the Church because he did not see himself a hero, and he loved life too much to die young. In Galileo's defense, unlike the real Spinoza (not Sobol's or Bursztyn's), he was a husband and father, and anyway, his heretical writings had made it safely across the border, so humanity had nothing to gain by his becoming a martyr.

[5] Eugene Falk, Renunciation as a Tragic Focus (Minneapolis: University of Minnesota Press), p. 54.

cause. After all, fanatics (in our times we think of Moslem Fundamentalist extremists) do not care about danger or loss of life; on the contrary, they welcome it. We know that for most religious fanatics the afterlife is much more appealing then the one lived here on earth.[6]

By contrast, the average, moderate hero is much more conflicted, more agonized when faced with serious or life and death decisions; hence, his sacrifice, if he decides to commit himself, is a tragic one. Galileo (both historical and Brecht's hero) decides to recant his heretical theory that the earth revolves around the sun to conform to church doctrine and save himself. It is rumored that right after recanting he could not control himself and whispered under his breath the now famous *"eppure is muove"* ("but it does go around.") Joan of Arc, another famous martyr and hero of countless dramatic works, at first recants, but later reneges and pays the price of death at the stake.[7]

Spinoza, however, is not in the same league. In his case, the worst that could happen was excommunication; still a man of strong passions—as Sobol presents him—he thinks twice before sacrificing everything dear to him for the higher cause. It is, therefore, not surprising that Sobol's hero does occasionally waver before finally deciding to stick to his statements and suffer the consequence. In a number of scenes Spinoza raises the possibility of recanting with his close Marrano friend,

---

[6] This notion of martyrdom, of willingly dying for a higher cause than life itself, is present among some Islamic fundamentalists in Iran and Shiite extremists waging "holy war" against Israel from Lebanon. In all cases, the one sacrificing his life, has usually very little to lose on earth, making the prospect of "eternal bliss" among the "holy martyrs" who gave their lives before him, very attractive. The Japanese WWII Kamikaze pilots on suicide missions against the enemy were fanatical as well, though they had a radically different mentality from the religious Moslem fanaticism.

[7] Joan of Arc is the protagonist of plays by Schiller, Brecht, Anouilh, Shaw, Anderson, and the main character in a number of films. While it is true that at first she recanted, in the end, unlike Galileo, she did go back on her recantation and died a true martyr in 1431, in Rouen, France.

Dr. Juan (Daniel) Prado, another heretic, but one who, unlike Spinoza, did recant twice. Prado does so because to him public image and acceptance is crucial; as a physician, he needs the community for his livelihood. Anyway, Prado finds it surprisingly easy to simply mouth the necessary words needed to placate the rabbis and *parnasim* and escape their wrath. Naturally, a man of strong principles like Spinoza cannot do so even though he is tempted by the prospects of a better life—a lucrative position in the community, funds to write his treatise, marriage, and a comfortable home.

In moments of despair, Spinoza seeks the council of his mentor, Rabbi Menashe ben Israel. Unfortunately, Menashe can offer little comfort as he had already "sold his soul to the Devil." Like Prado, he too retracted his unorthodox views. Thus, he tells Spinoza: "I was afraid. I was afraid to lose my position in the community. I gave in."[8] In Sobol's play, the greatest influence on the troubled scholar is not Prado or Rabbi Menashe, but a prostitute named Mary who, if only temporarily, manages to arouse his jealousy and tempt him into considering a new life in New Amsterdam, a life free of intellectual or religious constraints. But, in the end, Spinoza prefers a tortured life in Amsterdam over the prospects of a quieter, prosperous existence in America.

Though the interest in Spinoza continues to be strong among many Jewish intellectuals and scholars around the world, going to see a play about him in 1991, at Tel Aviv's prestigious "*Teatron Habima*" ("Habima National Theater"), signified much more than simply intellectual curiosity. The Spinoza case resonates for Israeli viewers in a special way. To them he is not merely a symbol of freedom of thought, but an admired fighter for freedom from religious authority, from rabbis and rabbinic

---

[8] Solo LeSpinoza, p. 83.

courts. To freethinking Israelis his opposition to Amsterdam's rabbis reminds them of their own ongoing opposition to religious coercion. These battles are not new. They have been waged since 1948 and there is no sign that they will go away soon. Watching Sobol's Spinoza they were reminded of the many intrusive prohibitions in their own daily lives, everything from laws governing *kashrut* to marriage and burial practices. Observing someone who dared take on the religious establishment must have felt good to these frustrated Israelis.

In sharp contrast to Sobol's serious treatment of the subject, Igal Bursztyn's film "Everlasting Joy" is a delightful romantic comedy about a certain Baruch Spinoza living in contemporary Tel Aviv. Like his namesake he too is a philosopher. He is a handsome bachelor in his late 30s, residing in a typical working-class apartment building in Tel Aviv. Though he has no job, he somehow manages to make a living. His neighbors include a drummer in a rock & roll band living with a oversexed Swedish tourist, a middle-aged couple with five children—she is a housewife, he works as a security agent in the territories—and another married couple without children.

This modern Spinoza spends most of his time writing controversial theories about God, the universe, knowledge, love, and just about anything that piques his interest. In fact, whenever one of his friends asks for advice, Spinoza is ready with neatly packaged statements, anecdotes, or sayings, some of which are actual quotes from the works of the original Spinoza of Amsterdam.

As the action unfolds, Spinoza witnesses a series of crises in human relationships: the childless couple breaks up—he commits suicide, she fantasizes making love to an athletic gym instructor—the Swede cheats on her partner with the very same instructor. Spinoza himself loses his beautiful Clara to a rotund and ugly doctor with lots of money. While everyone around him reacts emotionally, even violently, to these personal calamities, Spinoza manages to stay calm. Unlike his neighbors (by extension, many Israelis), Spinoza learns to control his feelings.

Thus, he argues that sadness and depression, emotions that go hand in hand with disappointment, are basically the result of ignorance, states of mind that reasonable, thinking people should learn to control—and can be controlled if only they used their brain.

In his eternal pursuit of everlasting joy he advocates moderation, reason and human compassion. In politics he is a liberal man, an activist for peace with the Arabs. As peace talks with Palestinians and other neighboring Arab states are showing only dim signs of any progress, he goes to the dangerous West Bank to negotiate a truce with leaders of the Hamas terrorist movement. Using personal charm and solid logic, he manages to convince them that the only answer to their problem is peaceful coexistence with Israel. At the end of the film, the same Arabs who earlier have been throwing stones at Israeli vehicles, are now driving freely through the streets of Tel Aviv. They are cheering and waving to the stunned crowds while heading for Spinoza's apartment to celebrate the new era of peace and understanding between Arabs and Jews.[9]

In many ways Baruch Spinoza is like his namesake from Amsterdam. He too lives alone, speaks his mind, defies authority, espouses humanitarian ideas, spurns materialism, and fights for individual rights. Unlike the original philosopher, this citizen of Tel Aviv (and by extension Israel's liberal Jews) emerges triumphant in his war against religious authority. His opposition to it brings him a great deal of

---

[9] A great deal has happened since Bursztyn's film premiered: several more rounds of negotiations followed by historic treaties, the assassination of Yitzhak Rabin, the death of King Hussein of Jordan. However, the breakthrough came at the 1990 Madrid Conference, when publically, Israeli and Arab leaders met face-to-face at the negotiating table.

discomfort, annoyance and loss of privacy. In one of the film's pivotal scenes, a scene fraught with symbolism, undercover agents hired by the rabbinate are positioned on rooftops across from Spinoza's apartment. They observe him day and night and listen in to his conversations. They also follow him on the streets.

After collecting sufficient material to pronounce him an apostate, the rabbinate sends a van equipped with loudspeakers to patrol the streets of the city and announce the excommunication orders. In addition to listing his heretical views, the announcement issues a warning against anyone trying to speak to or associate with him. While this is serious business, Bursztyn presents the material in a satiric, light comedic fashion; all attempts at gagging and isolating him only increase his popularity. His sex appeal is irresistible; his former girlfriend gets a divorce and returns to him; and the public at large hails him as a hero—while the Rabbis appear as fools trying in vain to shut him up.

By way of comedy, satire and surrealism, Bursztyn manages to create an unusually magical atmosphere, presenting us with a world where peace and harmony are not some dreams but a reality. This became possible because people listened to Spinoza and his logical reasoning. Anyone familiar with Israel and the Middle East knows that these qualities are foreign to the national character and cultures in the area. In a place where deep hatred and ancient grudges reign supreme, where conflicts are dealt with by resorting to emotions and passions, reason and moderation are a rare commodity. While events in the film are exaggerated, they reflect the hopes and aspirations of peace-loving Israelis and Palestinians on their way to a better future. While Igal Bursztyn was fortunate to witness the beginning of Israeli-Arab coexistence, he might not live to see another, more spectacular miracle—Jews living together in harmony.

Romance and Rambos: Hollywood and the Jewish State

The Jewish State declared independence over half a century ago, and Hollywood has not had much of intelligence to say about it since. "Exodus" (1960) and "Cast A Giant Shadow" (1966), two epics about the 1948 War of Independence, were enormously popular during a time when Israel enjoyed great world sympathy. Three subsequent films—"Victory at Entebbe" (1976), "Raid on Antebbe" (1977) and "Operation Thunderbolt" (1977)—followed the stunning 1976 Entebbe Operation in which an Israeli commando squad freed hijacked passengers from PLO terrorists. And in 1984, Amos Kollek, son of former Jerusalem mayor Teddy Kollek, produced, directed and starred in a negligible comedy called "Goodbye New York," about a young Manhattanite who ends up in Tel Aviv by mistake. Considering the prominence of Israel and the Middle East in global and American politics, it is amazing how little attention the Jewish State has received from the movie industry.

It is possible that producers consider Israel in the post-1967 War era to be too controversial, too risky an investment. They follow a long tradition of earlier movie moguls of the 1930s and 1940s, mainly Jews like Samuel Goldwyn, Louis Mayer and Sam Warner, who went out of their way to avoid Jews and Jewish themes in their works.[1] It seems that for America in the 1960s, the Israeli War of Independence was the only safe Jewish topic Hollywood could find: an ancient, persecuted nation rises from the devastation of World War II and Auschwitz, overcomes incredible odds, and establishes a free country on land promised by God. The war itself was already

---

[1] In the 1920s and 1930s Jews in Hollywood were under constant attack by American nativists, militant evangelicals and other right-wing antisemitic groups. No wonder that Jewish moguls like Sam Goldwyn tried their best to look, sound and act like good, loyal Americans. Any hint of Jewish favoritism or ethnic preference scared these movie producers to death. To make it here, these Jews felt they had to conform, assimilate, in short, to be more like their Waspish colleagues on the golf course. For a study of these Jewish producers, see: Neil Gable, An Empire of Their Own: How the Jews Invented Hollywood (New York: Doubleday, 1989), and a 1998 A&E TV documentary, "Hollywoodism, Jews, the Movies, and the American Dream."

remote enough. With the Cold War in full swing, Americans saw Israel as their only reliable Middle East ally, a sort of first line defense against Soviet aggression and expansionism. Most Americans viewed the establishment of the State of Israel in 1948 as a triumph of good over evil, of victims over oppressors, of few over many. The picture of the Holocaust survivor fighting for freedom and dignity evoked strong feelings. The decision to shoot "Exodus" and "Cast A Giant Shadow" in the 1960s may have been affected by the unprecedented success of two Biblical film epics of the 1950s: "The Ten Commandments"(1956) and "Ben Hur" (1959).[2]

As is the fate of many war movies, in "Exodus" and "Cast a Giant Shadow" too, history and politics become secondary as the personal interests—usually romantic—take center stage. While relations between the English, the Israelis, the United Nations and the Arabs, as well as the implications of the Holocaust on the Middle East, are touched upon to various degrees, in the end it is the love affairs between Ari Ben Canaan and Kitty, and between Colonel Marcus "Mickey" and Magda that become the focus of the films. In trying to balance the personal and historical material, producers were constrained by their inadequate literary resources: Leon Uris' overblown novel for "Exodus" and Ted Berkman's straightjacket biography of Mickey Marcus for "Cast A Giant Shadow."[3]

Despite a great deal of cutting, some critics still complained that the films were too long, too ambitious in their scope. Bosley Crowther of The New York Times, for one, writes that the creators of "Exodus" wanted to "embrace as much as

---

[2] The Jewish moguls felt comfortable with Biblical themes. Unlike the more parochial, often controversial, contemporary religious and ethnic issues, the universally respected Bible was a safe source of artistic inspiration.

[3] Leon Uris, Exodus (Garden City, NY: Doubleday, 1957); Ted Berkman, Colonel Mickey Marcus.

they could . . . first, the story of the ship 'Exodus' . . . then they wanted to follow the threads of several parallel plots involving an assortment of major characters . . . and finally, they wanted to tell something of the post-partition fight of the Jews against the Arabs."[4]

Kitty Fremont (Eva Marie Saint) of "Exodus" is an attractive, recently widowed American, a Presbyterian from Indiana whose husband, a photojournalist, has been killed somewhere in Palestine while on assignment. Early on, she debates if she should stay on or go back to the States. She seems to have lost all desire and ambition. Her best times are spent sipping afternoon tea with the entertaining General Sutherland (Sir Ralph Richardson), Commander of the British troops in Palestine. Her life takes an unexpected turn when, out of curiosity, she volunteers her medical expertise to help a group of Jewish illegal immigrants stranded on the ship "Exodus" in Haifa harbor. These Jews, mostly Holocaust survivors, are British prisoners, refugees of the colonial policy that restricted Jewish entry into Palestine. The policy was meant to preserve the Arab-Jew population balance in this hotly contested sliver of land.[5]

At this point the more discerning members of the audience might have noticed that something is amiss in the movie's perspective. Do Kitty's struggles deserve a place alongside the struggles of the survivors? Poor Kitty, the film makers seem to say, what a mess she's in—should she stay, bored, in this quaint Middle-Eastern land, or return to a lonely life of Indiana doldrums? Should we draw

---

[4]Bosley Crowter, The New York Times (December 16, 1960).

[5]The politics of colonial Britain, the Jews and the Arabs are covered in several excellent historical studies of the period. See: David Shipler, Arab and Jew: Wounded Spirits in a Promised Land (New York: Penguin Books, 1986); Walter Laqueur and Barry Rubin, The Israel-Arab Reader: History of the Middle East (New York: 1985); Howard Sachar, A History of Israel From the Rise of Zionism to Our Time (New York: Alfred A. Knopf,1979).

parallels between the miserable Holocaust survivors, once again and ever the victims, stranded on that horrid ship, and the agonizing Kitty? It certainly seems as we are expected to do so.

On the ship Kitty meets Ari Ben Canaan, a non-religious Jew with whom American audiences can easily relate, especially given what Lester Friedman calls, "his military daring, battlefield valor, and bland ethnicity."[6] This handsome, blue-eyed, Hagana fighter is the epitome of the Freedom Fighter: courageous, fanatical in his beliefs, dedicated to his people and cause, relentless in his pursuit of a dream. Being played by a smolderingly assimilated Jew like Paul Newman only adds to his vapid mystique. Ari's Jewishness amounts to little more than occasional biblical and historical references of the remember-that-time-during-the-Holocaust variety. Surely, Jewish Hollywood executives of the 1960s could identify with the type.

Mutatis mutandis, we could envision Ari as a guerrilla leader in a South American or Far Eastern setting, battling overwhelming odds in the form of a far more powerful colonial power. The difference is that here, in addition to the colonial power, the Hagana has to contend with militant Palestinians, opposing underground factions like the Irgun and the Stern Gang, and the might of neighboring Arab armies. It is precisely Ari's universal qualities, his "bland ethnicity," that make it possible for his romance with Kitty to upstage—incredibly—one of the most dramatic military struggles in recent world history. "Yes, it's true," to paraphrase the screenplay, "the Jews are about to return miraculously to sovereignty in their homeland after two thousand years of murderous exile, but Kitty, there's something terribly important I must tell you about the color of your eyes . . ."

---

[6]Lester Friedman, Hollywood's Image of the Jew (New York: Frederick Ungar, 1982), p. 192.

In fairness to Kitty, she knew self-sacrifice firsthand when she gave up her career for her husband, but is pleasantly surprised to learn that sacrifice for something larger can be so fulfilling. At the end of the film, gun poised in hand, she seems to have found a new life and a new home in Palestine, a place as different as one can imagine from her Midwestern roots. More than Ari's looks draw her to him—it is his self-confidence and strong sense of purpose that make him so lovable. Or maybe—the producers leave us wondering—it's that irresistible combination of destiny, spirituality and chutzpah that seals the fate of the future Mrs. Kitty Ben Canaan. Not once does anybody in the entire production seem bothered by the fact that Kitty is not Jewish. Why, after her husband's death, is she still here in this very dangerous place? What kind of a bureaucratic red tape awaits the gentile Ben Canaan in the new state's Interior Ministry? We may have to wait one day for "Exodus II" to find out.

In "Cast A Giant Shadow," Colonel Michael "Mickey" Marcus (Kirk Douglas), another American, this time a Jew, undergoes some radical personal changes as a result of his own involvement in Israel's War of Independence. This hero of WWII, a New York lawyer in civilian life, is now unhappy back at his job behind a desk. He misses the action, the sense of fulfillment from doing something historic, something that will change the world. His equally unhappy wife Emma (Angie Dickinson) quips that all he needs is "a good war" to give him satisfaction once more.

Mickey's unhappiness harms his marriage. For a long time he refuses to have children. When he finally gives in to Emma's entreaties, the pregnancy runs into complications. It is at this point that he is approached by the Hagana in New York to join the Jewish army's struggle for independence. Initially he is taken aback. Mickey is an assimilated Jew. (Hollywood favors the completely estranged or the most exaggerated ethnic type—rarely are middle-of-the-road committed Jews depicted). "My religion," he tells the Israelis, "is American. I went to Temple at thirteen for my Bar-Mitzvah, and once it was over, I was done with the Jews."

Mickey feels uneasy about leaving Emma with her difficult pregnancy, during a crisis time in their marriage, and so soon after his return from the war in Europe, but the excitement of fighting the good war in Palestine is too powerful to resist. A new battlefield awaits, as does the possibility of building a new army from scratch. He joins the effort and, after reaching the Holy Land, his domestic problems recede into the background. And just as the film begins to move from the banality of Mickey's personal soap opera to the spectacle of national rebirth, the scriptwriters become apprehensive and send in Magda (Germany's sexy Senta Berger), the proverbially strapping Israeli young woman who starts flirting with Mickey the moment he arrives at Lod Airport. "Quick," one can imagine the misogynystic banter in the script room, "things are turning dangerously consequential, bring in the seductive woman."

At first, even the smell of gunpowder and Magda's seductive powers don't seem to rouse Mickey from his distractions. Mickey is still searching for something; he has been restless for so long. And the Jews, they have been homeless for so long. We recall that Kitty too has been wandering aimlessly for so long. (Splice "Cast a Giant Shadow" and "Exodus" together and see if anyone notices the difference.) Apparently, in Europe when the war was winding down and American troops were freeing Holocaust survivors in Germany and Poland, Mickey tried desperately to be everywhere at the same time, before anyone else. His superior officer, General Mike Randolph (John Wayne, of course), becomes enraged with his recklessness in a famous confrontation scene. What was bothering Mickey? We never learn.

Fortunately, the struggling Jewish army captures his heart. He is drawn into the mission to fight, to become part of destiny, to fall for the stunning woman soldier. And what, after all this, is the climax of Mickey's self-actualization on the battlefield? Faithful to the real Marcus, the film makers are forced to kill the tortured soul in an unfortunate accident. The fact that he dies when he does is actually a godsend, since any other scenario would have placed them too far out of their depth. Would he have stayed in the Jewish land for good, a reclaimed lost Jew? Would he have unearthed his psychological demons? Would he have left his wife for the exotic Israeli? It was, no doubt, easier to leave Mickey as an unrequited martyr than to tie up any of his more substantive or philosophical loose ends. The only salient point that remains: the sight of proud and determined Israelis fighting against overwhelming odds is inspiring to a neurotic Jew.[7]

To date, neither the 1956 Sinai Campaign, the 1967 Six Day War, nor the 1973 Yom Kippur War have generated any American films. The daring 1976 Israeli raid on the Entebbe Airport in Uganda, however, has inspired Hollywood and Israeli producers alike. Unlike the other military conflicts, this action generated little controversy: a defensive, and of course successful, strike at hijacking thugs who threaten "innocent civilians" was the kind of family entertainment the whole world could stomach. More so since the story also involved a great deal of non-Israelis, including the Air France staff that had been navigating the routine flight from Tel Aviv to Paris.

Like "Exodus" and "Cast a Giant Shadow" before, the three major films— "Victory at Entebbe," "Raid on Antebbe" and "Operation Thunderbolt"—feature

---

[7] One reviewer, Wilfred Mifflin, wrote that "Cast a Giant Shadow" "even as propaganda for Israel, is of dubious value." Films in Review (No. 5, May, 1966). Some critics, however, were more positive about the film. See: Variety (March 30, 1966) (unsigned); and Charles Aaronson, Motion Pictures Herald (No. 13, April, 1966).

Israelis as the paratroopers ("good guys") and Arabs as the villains, this time accompanied by a collaborating team of Ugandans led by the eccentric figure of Israeli-trained Field Marshall Idi Amin Dada and a couple of German Baden-Manheim terrorists.

"Victory at Entebbe" (1976) is the most self-consciously sensationalist Hollywood product, directed by Marvin Chomsky, and featuring a circus-like array of mainly old-time performers like Burt Lancaster, Elizabeth Taylor, a resurrected Kirk Douglas, Anthony Hopkins, and the thankfully exorcized Linda Blair. The 1970s happened to be crop years for the airline/airport film genre, and the producers were not about to pass up on an opportunity to cash in on their popularity.

A slightly subdued approach was attempted in "Raid on Antebbe" (1977), directed by Irwin Kerschner, with the expressionless Charles Bronson—a favorite among army-obsessed Israelis for his shoot-first-ask-later Westerns—as well as the sinister German actor Horst Buchholtz. The same year, "Operation Thunderbolt" also appeared. Produced and directed in America by Menachem Golan with the support and approval of the Israeli government and army, the cast included Israeli stars Yehoram Gaon and Assaf Dayan (son of Moshe), and Klaus Kinski, another scary German actor. With the expensive casts in each film, subject matter must have overridden financial considerations, or maybe the surefire formula gave the producers an undue surge of confidence.

The storyline barely wavers between any of the films. Once again, Jews find themselves in an impossible situation, prisoners of brutal terrorists, a thousand miles from home, in the heart of Africa. And once again, adding to the drama is the shadow of the Holocaust, a subject whose lucrative possibilities are pushed to ever bizarre limits: as Jews confront a near certain death in the African airport, survivors display tattooed numbers to their captors. We may be in Uganda, and the hijacking-

Holocaust analogy may be ludicrous, but those familiar and ubiquitous numbers turn up anyway to add dramatic punch.

The hero, the one tragic military casualty of the action, is a handsome, American-educated Yonathan "Yoni" Netanyahu, a name that had been well known long before his brother Bibi entered Israeli politics. Though few action films appeared with Israelis as main characters, a host of other movies in the late 1970s and 1980s also feature Arabs as terrorists, targets of American commando raids on their training camps in Northern Africa or Lebanon. These works came in response to a rash of hijacks and other terrorist acts in Israel, the Middle East, and Europe. Americans remember best the hijacking of TWA Flight 847 in Athens and the capture of Achille Lauro, a cruise ship with American tourists, including Jews, in the Mediterranean. However, while the Entebbe operation ended in crushing victory, other terrorist acts concluded with mixed, even tragic results.

The reasonably well-made "Black Sunday" (1977), also of the action genre, features an Israeli hero, a Mossad agent who follows a terrorist (Marthe Keller, German as well) to America and kills her virtually seconds before she and a psychotic pilot (a very intense Bruce Dern) explode a blimp over a Super Bowl-crowded stadium. Film historian W. Palmer points out that the "terrorist of the late 70s is a wronged individual pursuing a revenge scenario who has allowed himself to become the tool of some deeply backgrounded, unnamed political cause..."[8] In this case, the woman, trained by radical Palestinian forces, is terrorizing America because it supports Israel; the pilot is settling accounts with the army over its handling of his Vietnam record.

---

[8]William Palmer, Films of the 1980s (Carbondale: Southern Illinois University Press, 1990), p. 120.

Had the macho Israeli come of age in America cinema, or was he just the logical foil to a more popular Arab or German caricature that audiences just loved to hate? Not a question of consequence in fickle Hollywood, as the "good guy vs. bad guy" dichotomies would morph into American-Russian, American-Japanese, and even American-Iranian dyads, depending on the popular culture's preference in global tensions during any given year.

An Israeli named Amos Kollek tried to change this one-dimensional image of Israelis in Hollywood with his comedy, "Goodbye New York" (1984). His English-speaking formula piece for American consumption stars Julie Hagerty—fresh from her own "Airport" spoofs in the irreverent "Airplane" (1980) and "Airplane II" (1982)—as Nancy Callahan, a cheated wife on the lark.

Unfortunately, Kollek only manages to make another side of Israeli life appear monolithic. No longer the burly officers or victimized survivors of earlier films, the Israelis that Nancy encounters during her misadventures in the Jewish state are buffoons of all shapes and sizes: urbanites, kibbutzniks, soldiers, opportunists, thieves, louts. The cast of characters is artificially colorful, quirky and pandering.

Like Kitty and Mickey, Nancy arrives in Israel on the heels of personal problems (perhaps this is movieland's ultimate vision for the Jewish state, a kind of therapeutic dreamland for the forlorn). One day, after quitting her dull job, she rushes home on a romantic whim to persuade her husband to travel with her to Paris. She runs into their apartment and, in her flawless cinematic timing, finds her mate with another woman. After an unamusing confrontation, Nancy decides to go on the trip by herself, hoping that Paris will provide refuge from her marital woes. Too many sleeping pills in the air, and the next thing she knows she has missed her stop, landing instead in Tel Aviv. And as luck would have it, she finds she is without luggage, clothes, money or credit cards, and of course she is too proud to ask her philandering husband for money. So, there she is, poor Nancy—stranded, the victim of a terribly contrived plot device.

Almost immediately, she is accosted by a host of sleazy Israeli men who try to seduce her: a playboy who picks her up in a boat on the Kineret, a boyfriend of her roommate on a kibbutz, a camel rider who wants an American wife to add to his already large harem of females. Nancy seems to really get around the country—remarkable on her budget—but all the Israelis she meets seem variations on the same theme, comic relief from weak comedy. Finally she hooks up with David (Amos Kollek himself), a divorced history teacher, the inevitable nice guy in the group. After a predictable series of madcap misunderstandings, David demonstrates his down-home Middle Eastern hospitality by buying a plane ticket for Nancy to return to New York. She reciprocates by "showing him a good time."

Nancy has learned from the Israelis to loosen up, to take things in stride, especially relationships. The lovemaking in the car, near the airport, is her way of showing David how much she has changed in Israel. The frustrated wife and bored professional from urban America finally finds release in Israel's free-spirited society. A change of pace from the stiff macho characters of earlier films? Perhaps. In the end, however, the viewer hardly feels that Kollek has shared a genuine slice of Israeli culture; he has merely reworked old caricatures and stereotypes to further his comedic plot.

Hollywood presented formulaic war adventures in the 1960s, Entebbe daredevils in the 1970s, while Kollek made us laugh with his 1980s light comedy. On the whole, American spectators have not been able to view more than cultural stereotypes and one-dimensional heroes. Life in Israel proper, with all its drama and conflicts, is still waiting for a more sophisticated English-language cinematic treatment.

Israeli films have, so far, failed to make inroads into mainstream or even Jewish-American entertainment markets the way Italian or Irish cinema has.[9] Irish or Italian works draw relatively large crowds of various ethnic makeup. If, for a moment, we restrict ourselves to the Jewish public, we will find that unlike the Italian or the Irish, the Jews are culturally and emotionally more connected to their ancestral roots in Eastern Europe than to their national Middle-Eastern homeland. To be sure, this is the only Jewish country in the world, but sadly, it is still culturally alien to most Americans, Jews and Gentiles alike. This, to some extent, explains the popularity of "Yentl," Holocaust films, or films with Jewish themes set in Europe.

---

[9] So far, no Israeli film has had a successful commercial run in this country. Some works, like Gila Almagor's "The Summer of Avia," about Holocaust survivors in the early years in Israel, and her sequel, "Under the Domim Tree," about immigrant youth during those years, have been shown in small art theaters around the country. Some recent releases—"Kadosh," "A Time of Favor" and "Late Marriage"—have also been shown in some prestigious art theaters (New York City's Lincoln Plaza Cinemas, for one) and have received a fair amount of critical attention. Once a year, in New York and Los Angeles, "The Israel Film Festival" presents new works from Israel. On Israeli films, see: Ella Shohat, Israeli Cinema: East/West and the Politics of Representation (Austin: University of Texas Press, 1989); Amy Kronish, World Cinema-Israel (Cranbury, NJ: Associated University Press, 1996).

Major Shoah Films: When Exception is the Rule

A typical Shoah story goes something like this: a simple Jew, probably a small-time merchant living in a small East European town, is forced by the Fascist authorities to pack his bags and move to a ghetto, usually in a larger town. After a while, he is deported to a concentration camp where he is separated from family and friends. Ghetto life prepares him for some of the hardships he encounters in the camps; however, survival depends on many factors not the least of which is sheer luck. So, if he somehow manages to avoid selection, and is sufficiently strong to withstand constant mental and physical punishments, he might survive. This story, multiplied thousands of times with minor variations, is what characterizes the plight of European Jews during the Second World War. While a horrifying tale, it lacks the necessary dramatic qualities—conflict, clash of ideas or values—the kind of stuff that goes into the making of good, tragic drama.[1]

In the hands of such extraordinary narrative practitioners as Primo Levi and Elie Wiesel, this otherwise "undramatic" material does succeed in engaging us, in some strange way, even "please" us.[2] The medium of theater and film, on the other hand, is much more dependent on material that can best be characterized as problematic, controversial, shocking or strange. Narratives have more freedom in what can or cannot be said; for sheer practical reasons, the medium of film and theater is limited in what it shows and how it shows it. The problematics of Shoah representation in both biographical or fictionalized narratives, as well as in dramatic

---

[1] Irving Howe made this comment in a paper delivered at a SUNY Albany-sponsored conference, "Writing and the Holocaust," April 5-7, 1987. The papers appeared in a book edited by Berel Lang, Writing and the Holocaust, (NY: Holmes & Meier, 1988), p. 189. Says Howe: "The exterminations...have little drama in them. Terribleness, yes; drama, no."

[2] I am mainly referring to Levi's and Wiesel's autobiographical works Survival in Auschwitz and Night, respectively. In both, literary devices are used to heighten the drama and engage the reader.

and visual arts, have triggered a great deal of critical literature. (See "Works Consulted," at end of this chapter.)

It is, therefore, not surprising that three of the most successful Shoah films of the last fifteen years have been those that opted for the atypical, even the bizarre: "Sophie's Choice" (1982) focuses on the suffering of a Polish-Catholic woman mistakenly deported to Auschwitz; "Europa, Europa" (1991) follows the adventures of Solomon Prel, a Polish Jew who survives the war by pretending to be an Aryan; "Schindler's List" (1993), another true story, is about a German businessman in Cracow who saves Jews by employing them in his factory. Set against the grim background of the war or of the ghettoes and concentration camps, these unusual plots are indeed the stuff of "good drama."

"Sophie's Choice," the screen version of William Styron's enormously popular novel by the same title, was directed by Alan Pakula, and features two of Hollywood's favorite actors—Meryl Streep as Sophie Zawistowska and Kevin Kline as Nathan Landau. In 1978, Meryl Streep portrayed a similar role in the NBC television drama "Holocaust"; on the smaller screen she plays Inga, the Catholic wife of a deported German Jew. The drama for this groundbreaking show is provided by the unusual, only marginally relevant fact that during the war mixed couples and some gentiles too suffered from the Nazi racist policies. While in "Holocaust" the Gentile wife suffers the pain of separation from her Jewish husband, in "Sophie's Choice" she must endure both, the horrors of Auschwitz as well as the weight of a guilty conscience: soon after arrival in the concentration camp, Sophie is forced to choose which one of her two children should live. Sophie's camp experience, like the plot in general, is atypical: her pure Aryan looks and fluent German land her a job as secretary to the camp commandant. As such, she is fed and cared for much better than any Jewish prisoner could ever have dreamed.

After liberation Sophie ends up in Brooklyn, where, through another set of strange circumstances, she falls in love with Nathan Landau, an American Jew. He is an attractive intelligent man. The problem is that Nathan is a drug addict, a paranoid and a schizophrenic. It seems that his deep emotional problems stem from feelings of guilt for having lived in safety, in America, while the Holocaust was taking place in Europe.

To cope with his guilty conscience, Nathan collects Holocaust paraphernalia—books, movies, music, artifacts—all crammed into one room where Nathan tries to recreate through sight and sound the horrors of his European coreligionists. The relationship is no less bizarre: while in love with Sophie the woman, he loathes everything she represents: the Polish gentiles who assisted the Nazis in exterminating the Jews, the Pole who lives while most Jews died. As the surviving Polish "shiksa," Sophie is the perfect punching bag for Nathan's deep neurosis: she must pay for the death and suffering of the millions who perished. As for Sophie, not only did she suffer unjustly in Poland, she continues to suffer in New York, ironically, at the hands of a pathologically vindictive Jew. This love-hate relationship eventually leads to a double suicide, a fitting ending for two tortured souls who could not find respite from a guilty conscience and haunting ghosts of the past.

This bizarre, often perverse relationship, and Sophie's Auschwitz experience serve as perfect vehicle for the film's stars, especially for the versatile Meryl Streep who had to speak in a Polish accent throughout. Janet Maslin of The New York Times, for example, feels that Meryl Streep "offers a performance of such measured intensity that the results are by turns exhilarating and heartbreaking."[3] "The film,"

---

[3] Janet Maslin, The New York Times (December 10, 1982).

she goes on to say, "casts a powerful, uninterrupted spell."⁴ Sheila Benson of The Los Angeles Times echoes those sentiments by noting that "the role of Sophie, its beautiful, complex, worldly heroine, gives Meryl Streep the chance at bravura performance and she is, in a word, incandescent."⁵ While even this much Auschwitz, violence and perverse sex might offend certain viewers, "Sophie's Choice" is relatively tame when compared with some other Holocaust works that clearly exploit such tantalizing mixtures for pure commercial reasons. I am thinking of Liliana Cavani's "The Night Porter" (1974), and Lina Wertmuller's "Seven Beauties" (1975), as two well known examples of this controversial way of depicting the Holocaust.⁶

While I agree that Streep's and Kline's performances are outstanding, I find the plot contrived; the Auschwitz scenes, while striving for a sense of vraisemblance, come off as rather fake. However, what troubles me most is what Phyllis Deutsch of Jump Cut correctly describes as "the suffering of the Jews always remains peripheral to Sophie's story."⁷ She explains: "When Sophie visits the Jewish ghetto in Cracow, and later, when she stands in line at Auschwitz, the camera focuses on Meryl Streep's beautiful blondness. In both scenes the Jews huddle together in the background, dark and indistinguishable, smaller than Streep, smaller than life . . . Sophie stands somewhat apart . . . she is not one of them . . . she cries out to a guard,

---

⁴Ibid.

⁵Sheila Benson, The Los Angeles Times, December 10, 1982.

⁶For an in-depth analysis of "The Night Porter" and "Seven Beauties," see Insdorf's discussion in her Indelible Shadows.

⁷Phyllis Deutsch, Jump Cut, No.29, February 1984.

'I am a Christian, I'm not a Jew.'"[8] Respected critic Andrew Sarris of The Village Voice echoes some of Deutsch's concerns. Basically, he argues that the movie/book tend to trivialize the Holocaust; by choosing a Polish Sophie, the daughter of a Polish anti-Semite. Styron, says Sarris, "makes her an ideally ironic victim from virtually every point of view."[9] I would only add that the choice of a Polish-Catholic hero does indeed make the story of the Holocaust so much more dramatic, more universal, thus much more appealing to a wider reading/viewing audience. As Ilan Avisar summed it up, Styron's narrative was designed "to downplay the victimization of the Jews in order to drive home the universalization of the Holocaust."[10]

While I find this trend disturbing, many film critics, as well as some leading American Jewish figures, have viewed this type of message to be a positive one. In her analysis of the NBC-TV "Holocaust—The Miniseries," a work featuring similar themes as "Sophie's Choice," a critic, Judith Doneson, argues that "the show 'Holocaust' has made the history of the destruction of European Jewry a part of the American consciousness, both Christian and Jewish. The memory of the event belongs to the American people, to be refreshed annually, to be commemorated in the nation's capital, absorbed as part of its own history."[11] Finally, to bolster her argument, she cites Rabbi Mark Tenenbaum, who stated in 1978 that "Holocaust" has brought the message as nothing else has—neither books, lectures, documentaries—to some 200 million people in 50 countries throughout the world. It is a message on which the very survival of the human family depends in a nuclear missile age, an age

---

[8]Ibid.

[9]Andrew Sarris, The Village Voice (December 28, 1982).

[10]Avisar, p. 127.

[11]Doneson, p. 196

which for the first time is able to conceive of a global Auschwitz."[12]

While the plot in Styron/Pakula is invented, the one in Agnieszka Holland's "Europa, Europa" is based on a true story. The film is a screen recreation of Solomon Perel's autobiography.[13] Perel, played by Marco Hofschneider, was born in 1925 near Hannover, Germany. In 1935 he flees with his family to Lodz to avoid Nazi persecutions. However, four years later, they eventually catch up with him in Poland. Together with his older brother, they flee again; they become separated, with Solomon ending up in a Communist boarding school in Russian-occupied Western Poland. There, he learns Russian and the basics of Leninist/Stalinist doctrine.

In 1941 the Germans take over the area; to escape death Solomon declares himself a Volksdeutscher (an ethnic German), joins the German army, and accidentally commits an act of heroism for which he is decorated and sent to an elite Hitler Youth Nazi camp in Braunschweig. Solomon, who changes his name to Josef Peters, or "Jupp" to his friends, is close to being adopted by a childless officer, is revered by his German peers, and is almost seduced by Leni (Julie Delpy), the daughter of a war hero, a fallen officer from the collapsing Russian front. When the Russians take over Germany, Solomon reveals his true identity to the liberators who find his services valuable since he is fluent in both Russian and German. After the war he emigrates to Palestine, and at the present time he is still alive in Israel.

A Jew masquerading as a Nazi? What could be more dangerous? And what could be more fraught with irony? On the dangerous side, Solomon must avoid showers, physicals and sexual encounters, even if the willing party is the beautiful daughter of a high German officer, a hero who died on the Russian front. The irony

---

[12]Ibid.

[13]Solomon Preil, I Was A Nazi Youth.

is present whenever racial slurs are heard, or songs joyfully announcing the "sharpening of knives to kill Jews" are sung in noisy beer halls or by triumphantly marching military convoys. To cap it all off, Solomon is showcased in a lecture about race, particularly at the point where the major differences between the "inferior" Slavs and Jews and the "pure, superior" Nordic/Aryan are underscored. According to the "race expert," physical attributes immediately give away the identity of the subject; this, more than anything else, demarcates the two groups.

As we learn from Jack Zipes, a scholar of German Jewry, these "scientifically proven" racial ideas are not new with the Nazis; they are deeply rooted in German culture. Throughout history they constitute a source of tension and identity crisis among many of Germany's assimilation-prone Jews. This, then, according to Zipes, is one of the major themes in Holland's film: "the Jew's body as a site of operations to demarcate what purity and beauty should be according to the majority German Aryan model is the major topical image for Holland."[14]

Amazingly, Solomon succeeds to fool just about anyone. He does so chiefly because he is very childlike, naive, a kind of Forrest Gump, a Chamaeleo, or as David Danby so aptly put it, a "Jewish Pasqualino," the main hero and endearing clown of Lina Wertmuller's controversial Holocaust film, "Seven Beauties."[15] Ironically, the one who sees through Solomon's playacting and discovers his true identity is himself playing a deadly role; he is a homosexual German soldier, a former actor who befriends this Polish Marrano. Survival then is the capacity to adapt, even to radically change, as the situation warrants. If we accept Solomon as a metaphor

---

[14]Jack Zipes's analysis of the film, "The Contemporary German Fascination for Things Jewish: Toward a Jewish Minor Culture," is in Sander Gilman and Karen Demmler, eds., Reemerging Jewish Culture in Germany (NY: New York University Press, 1994).

[15]David Denby, New York Magazine (July 15, 1991).

for Jewish existence and survival, his experience demonstrates the complete opposite of what we have been traditionally led to believe, namely that Jews survived because in all facets of life—religion, language, customs—they tried desperately, often at great peril, to act differently from the people around them. But then, Perel's situation and "Europa, Europa" are far from anything typical about Jewish experience and history.

While mildly interesting as a dark satire of racism and anti-Semitism, "Europa, Europa" is only peripherally a film about Jewish suffering in the Holocaust. While it is true that the signs for the outbreak of all-out atrocities are there—violence against Jews, the bloody pogrom in Lodz during Solomon's Bar-Mitzvah—the full-blown destruction is kept out of sight. A personal, deeply touching moment, however, does take place at least once. Dressed as a German soldier, Solomon travels by streetcar through the Lodz ghetto; he tries to peek through the blacked out windows for a glimpse of his family or friends. An old woman appears near a building. He thinks she is his mother, but, under these extraordinary circumstances, he cannot leave the tram car to find out. He must remain still even if it turns out that it is her. In the end, like Sophie, Perel too is one very lucky person having survived the hell of Nazi-orchestrated terrors.

I begin my discussion of Steven Spielberg's "Schindler's List" with a statement by Jeffrey Katzenberg, head of the "Disney Film Studios," a close friend and partner of Spielberg's. Soon after the film was released, he said this of his friend's creation: "I think 'Schindler's List' will wind up being so much more important than a movie. It will affect how people on this planet think and act. At a moment in time, it is going to remind us about the dark side, and do it in a way in which, whenever that little green monster is lurking somewhere, this movie is going to press us down again. I think it will bring peace on earth, good will to men."[16] At the other extreme we find Art Spiegelman of Maus: A Survivor's Tale fame who says: "The film is not about Jews, or arguably, even the Holocaust. Jews make people uncomfortable. It's about the benign aspects of capitalism with a human face. We're in Ayn Rand country: the businessman as hero. Capitalism can give us a health care program, and it can give us a Schindler."[17]

In the middle, we find critics like James Young. He does find some virtues in the film—mainly raising consciousness about the Shoah—while at the same time expressing some concerns that the film could possibly become a sort of final statement, a kind of permanent monument for the events "wiping out 34 years of other really interesting films on the Holocaust."[18]

I do share Young's partially positive view of the film, for, as we all know, nothing, not even NBC's immensely popular "Holocaust," generated as much discussion and debates (even full-fledged conferences) as has Spielberg's film. In addition, "Schindler's List" provided the impetus and most likely the finances for Spielberg's other major Holocaust project—the "Survivors of the Shoah Visual History Foundation," an organization set up to videotape the story of every living survivor in the world (so far, over 50,000). These memoirs—pictures and narratives— are preserved on highly sophisticated computer CD technology, and are made available to schools, libraries and a variety of research institutions around the world. "The Shoah Foundation" is also behind the critically acclaimed 1999

---

[16] Katzenberg's comments appear in a special issue of The Village Voice (March 29, 1994) devoted to criticism of "Schindler's List."

[17] Ibid.

[18] Ibid.

documentary, "The Last Days" about Hungarian survivors returning to Auschwitz 50 years later.[19] As to Young's worries, it took only five years and a most unlikely artist—Roberto Benigni, an Italian comedic actor—to produce "Life is Beautiful" (1997), reminding us that the Shoah remains an inexhaustible source of creative imagination, that nothing, not even "Schindler's List" could bring closure to it.[20]

It is very difficult to fault a work of this magnitude and cultural impact; nonetheless, Spielberg's "Schindler's List" is first and foremost a film about Oskar Schindler, a German industrialist who, when caught up in the Nazi madness, ends up in the Cracow ghetto, raises sufficient funds to retool a broken down textile factory, obtains the necessary permits, and begins producing cost-effective ammunition for the German army. The low cost is the result of employing Jewish slave labor instead of Polish or German workers. What starts as a purely business arrangement between Schindler and the Nazi officials gradually becomes a crusade to save as many Jews as possible by keeping them employed at his Cracow plant. This transformation is basically a reaction to the daily horror he witnesses in war-ravaged Poland—beatings, humiliation, hunger, the roundups and eventual deportation of Jews to Auschwitz. Schindler is the "good German" who refuses to take part in the slaughter. It is true that Schindler had relatively little to fear. A well-connected businessman in the Nazi elite circles, he had the perfect excuse: what he did was not for the Jews but for the Wehrmacht, especially when Germany needed it most—in the 1943-44 period with the Russian front slowly but surely collapsing in the East. Even so, Schindler undertook some pretty risky measures to help his workers stay alive.

---

[19]"The Last Days" won the 1999 Oscar for a documentary, five years after "Schindler" received multiple Oscars, including "Best Film" and "Best Director" for Spielberg.

[20]Roberto Benigni's "Life is Beautiful" brought him "Best Actor" honors at the 1999 Oscars. Debates about the film still rage years after its appearance.

In the end, noble motives or not, Schindler saves over a thousand people, and that is what matters most. To be sure, Spielberg insists that we do not think of Schindler as a saint. By showing us Schindler's human failings—his drinking, carousing—Spielberg seems to be suggesting that even an "imperfect hero," even a morally flawed man like Schindler, was capable of distinguishing between good and evil while ready to take action on behalf of the Jews. According to Daniel Goldhagen, Germans were capable of doing what they did because of something uniquely inherent in their culture, including blind obedience to authority.[21] If that is true, how do we explain Schindler's behavior? It must be that moral choices were available, and some, like an imperfect Schindler, refused to follow the herd and did what they could under extreme circumstances.

Aside from this valuable moral lesson, what does the film teach about the Shoah? Like in "Sophie's Choice," the suffering Jews appear mostly in the background. They move to the foreground when violence erupts; and when it does so, violence is graphic as prisoners are tortured, killed and raped directly in front of the camera. In general, the mix of sex and sadistic violence is a rather disturbing feature in this film. In seeking realism, Spielberg is walking a dangerously tight rope, for as Geoffrey Hartman points out, this sort of stark cinematic realism (black and white as opposed to color) can produce the opposite of the desired affect of horror and repulsion—"a numbing of sensibilities and even perverse, voyeuristic, pleasure."[22] These are very difficult matters to ascertain since no two viewers see things the same way; also, it is hoped that most experienced viewers are capable of

---

[21]Daniel Goldhagen, <u>Hitler's Willing Executioners</u>. The author's assertion that the evil emanating from Germany was primarily a culturally-defined phenomenon keeps alive the debate about responsibility and guilt.

[22]Geoffrey Hartman, "The Cinema Animal: On Spielberg's Schindler's List," <u>Yale Studies</u>.

adopting the necessary aesthetic distance in order to feel empathy while protecting themselves from emotional injury.

Despite these reservations, I do fear that inadvertently "Schindler's List" can evoke the wrong response in some viewers. Nonetheless, of the three films discussed here, "Schindler's List" is the most explicit in its depiction of Jewish suffering and death in the Shoah. However, like "Europa, Europa," this story too ends on a positive note—Jews are saved. True to history (and the books on which they were based), these works show us Solomon Perel living happily in Israel while "Oskar Schindler's Jews" have by now lived to see over six thousand of their offspring grow up in freedom in Israel and America.

But, as noted earlier, truth or not, the overwhelming typical Shoah story is one of total misery and death, not of life and redemption; the typical story, though, lacks the drama and tragedy present in the unusual lives, invented or true, of Sophie Zawistowska, Solomon Perel and Oskar Schindler. Sadly, to experience the typical, we must be prepared to submit to Claude Lanzmann's unremitting nine hours of his monumental "Shoah," or black and white documentaries like Alain Resnais's "Night and Fog."

Works Consulted

See: Sidra Ezrachi, *By Words Alone: The Holocaust in Literature* (Chicago: University of Chicago Press, 1980); James Young, *Writing and Rewriting the Holocaust: Narrative and the Consequences of Interpretation* (Bloomington: Indiana University Press, 1990); *The Texture of Memory: Holocaust Memorials and Meaning* (New Haven: Yale University Press, 1993); Alvin Rosenfeld, *A Double Dying: Reflections on Holocaust Literature* (Bloomington: University of Indiana Press, 1980); Saul Friedlander, ed., *Probing the Limits of Representation: Nazism and the*

Final Solution (Cambridge: Harvard University Press, 1992).; Lawrence Langer, *The Holocaust and the Literary Imagination* (New Haven:Yale University Press, 1975); *Versions of Survival: The Holocaust and the Human Spirit* (Albany: SUNY Press, 1982); *Admitting the Holocaust* (NY: Oxford University Press, 1995); *Preempting the Holocaust* (New Haven: Yale University Press,1998); Berl Lang's (already mentioned) *Writing and the Holocaust* and his recent books, *The Future and Post-Holocaust* (Bloomington: Indiana University Press, 2004); Daniel Schwarz, *Imagining the Holocaust* (New York: St. Martin's Press, 1999); Gary Weissman, *Fantasies of Witnessing* (Ithaca: Cornell University Press, 2004).

Discussions of the implications for drama and theater are found in: Edward Isser, *Stages of Annihilation: Theatrical Representations of the Holocaust* (Madison, NJ: Fairleigh Dickinson University Press, 1997); Elinor Fuchs, ed., *Plays of the Holocaust* (NY: Theater Communications Group, 1987); Robert Skloot, *The Darkness We Carry: The Drama of the Holocaust* (Madison: University of Wisconsin Press, 1988); Michael Taub, ed., *Israeli Holocaust Drama* (Syracuse; Syracuse University Press, 1996); Claude Schumacher, ed., *Staging the Holocaust* (NY: Cambridge University Press, 1998).

Book-length studies of cinema and the Shoah are: Ilan Avisar, *Screening the Holocaust: Cinema's Images of the Unimaginable* (Bloomington: Indiana University Press, 1988); Annette Insdorf, *Indelible Shadows: Film and the Holocaust* (Cambridge: Cambridge University Press, 1983); and Judith Doneson, *The Holocaust in American Film* (Philadelphia: The Jewish Publication Society, 1987).

On the impact of the Holocaust on American life and culture, see: Jeffrey Shandler, *While America Watches: Television and the Holocaust* (Oxford University Press, 1999); Peter Novick, *The Holocaust in American Life* (New York: Houghton Mifflin, 1999); Alan Mintz, *Popular Culture and the Shaping of Holocaust Memory in America* (Seattle: University of Washington Press, 1991); Hilene Flantzbaum, *The Americanization of the Holocaust* (Baltimore: Johns Hopkins University Press, 1999).

Minor Shoah Films: Fun And Games Allowed

In an attempt to create dramatic situations out of the dark night of the Shoah, some film makers have opted for the extraordinary, the unusual, for, as I mentioned in my other essay on the Holocaust, the typical Shoah story is missing the kind of drama that produces good movies or plays. It seems that as the old, mass murder century was coming to an end, directors' appetite for this risky and difficult subject was at its highest point. In America alone, no less than five Holocaust films had been released commercially in a short span of two years (1998-1999). In some ways these films are different from each other; however, they do share some similarities. Several seek to engage the audience through clever use of comedy: "Train of Life" (Radu Mihaileanu, 1997); "Life is Beautiful" (Roberto Benigni, 1998); and "Jacob the Liar" (Peter Kassovitz, 1999). Others— "Apt Pupil" (Bryan Singer, 1999) and "The Devil's Arithmetic" (Donna Deitch, 1999)—rely on elaborate plots designed primarily to educate the young on the lessons of the Shoah.

In Mihaileanu's "Train of Life," a village fool who learns about impending deportations convinces the shtetl's wise men to buy a train, fill it with people, including fake German guards, pretend it is a real transport of Jews, and travel in it to Russia and from there to Palestine. In Benigni's film, Guido, a good-natured Italian Jew (played by Benigni) and his son, cope with the horrors of the camps by pretending that all the terrible things happening to them are in fact part of an amusingly elaborate game. In "Apt Pupil," a film based on a Stephen King novella, a highschool student discovers a former Nazi officer (Ian McKellen) in his own Midwestern town; he befriends him, and together they engage in a series of bizarre events culminating in the old man's suicide. Based on a novel by Jane Yolen, "The Devil's Arithmetic" tells the story of another highschool student, Hannah (Kirsten Dunst) from New Rochelle, who, in "Wizard of Oz" fashion, is transported back in time to Poland and the Nazi death camps; she eventually returns a changed person.

The protagonist of "Jacob the Liar" is a former pancake peddler (Robin Williams); while in the ghetto, in 1944, he lies about having a radio and cheers everyone up with reports of German defeats and Allies' victories. This film is a remake of "Jacob der Lugner" (Frank Beyer, 1974), a German work based on Jurek Becker's novel, and nominated in 1977 for an Oscar for "Best Foreign Film."

Of all these new works, "Life is Beautiful" has received the most critical attention (only matched by Spielberg's "Schindler's List").[1] Critics and the public are divided between those who feel that using humor to show the Holocaust is both legitimate and effective, and those who feel that comedy is inappropriate, even insulting to the memory of the Shoah. I am not interested in arguing either side in this interesting debate; instead, I will touch on the film's treatment of history and its educational value.

Interviews with Benigni indicate that the Italian director/actor has consulted a number of historians and read a great deal of material before shooting the film.[2] In the same breath he confesses that the film is not about the Holocaust but about a person's strategies to survive in an extreme situation and that the Holocaust is the most extreme situation imaginable. The problem is that Benigni's story unfolds against the backdrop of 1940s Italy, and not in some vague or unidentifiable place and time, as is the case with some of the updated cinematic versions of Shakespeare's

---

[1] "Life is Beautiful" received an extraordinary amount of attention. Reviews appeared in all major newspapers and in popular periodicals. Benigni won prizes in Europe, Israel, and the "Oscar" in America. Abraham Foxman, the national director of the Anti-Defamation League and a survivor, defended Benigni and his use of humor and comedy to depict the events. (Jewish Standard, October 30, 1998).

[2] Benigni spoke about his research for the film in several published newspaper interviews. See: The Jerusalem Report (October 26, 1998); The Washington Post (November 1, 1998).

plays.³ As such, the film leaves itself open to legitimate scrutiny, which Benigni could have avoided had he chosen the same route as those Shakespearean films. Benigni knew very well that a film about a non-specified time and place, about abstract people in a tight spot, would have received little attention as compared to a film about the Shoah. Setting a film in the context of the Shoah creates interest and controversy which leads to media and public attention and ultimately to box office success.

In my argument I enlist the support of two distinguished critics, David Danby of The New Yorker and Jon Hoberman of The Village Voice. The question I am asking is, What do we learn about Italian Fascism from watching this movie? Denby points out that Benigni tries very hard to leave the impression that Italian Fascism was but an illusion, that it was "a form of buffoonery, and satire of it effectively diminishes it."⁴ As to Benigni's ridiculing the Fascists' false sense of power and control, Denby believes that the Italian director's fantastic ploys to counter the Fascists' own fantasy of control and power is "a sweet, noble idea, but, really, it's no more than a conceit."⁵ Those familiar with Fellini's "Amarcord" (1974) will no doubt recognize similarities between the old master's own comical, somewhat grotesque images of Fascism and Il Duce and that of the creator of "Life is Beautiful." Even with the best intentions, parodies of dictatorships and dictators are

---

³Italian cinema has dealt with the Fascist period and the Jewish question in other films as well. I have mentioned De Sica's "The Garden of the Finzi-Continis" (1971), Fellini's "Amarcord" (1974) and Zeffirelli's "Tea with Mussolini" (1999); others of note are Bernardo Bertolucci's "The Conformist" (1971) and Lina Wertmuller's "Seven Beauties" (1976). Susan Zuccotti's The Italians and the Holocaust (New York: Basic Books, 1987) is an excellent historical source on this subject.

⁴David Denby, "In the Eye of the Beholder: Another Look at Roberto Benigni's Holocaust Fantasy," The New Yorker (March 15, 1999).

⁵Ibid.

always problematic; it is not easy bringing evil to life through comedy and satire. Chaplin's 1940 classic, "The Great Dictator" is as close to success as any subsequent attempt at this risky cinematic genre.

Historical inaccuracies, however, are another issue. After careful analysis of Benigni's film, Hoberman points out that "Italian race laws forbade intermarriage, and by the time Guido is deported Italy had been at war for five years and was under German occupation. Indeed, Guido is unaware that most Italian Jews were rounded up and sent to Auschwitz during the winter of 1943-44."[6] Other inaccuracies include the film's camp scenes, the fact that the action takes place in an abandoned factory, and that the barracks are housed in a converted warehouse with prisoners and guards looking more like characters in a television sitcom series than inmates in a concentration camp.

I am not totally against Benigni's use of comedy. What I do object to is his characterization of the events, his distortion of historical facts, his strategy of fending off criticism by calling the film a "fable," and not a realistic representation of a historical moment. Most viewers, absorbed in the heart wrenching drama of survival, of fatherly devotion and love, are no doubt unaware of these problems. In comparison, another war-time Italian film, Vittorio De Sica's "The Garden of the Finzi Continis" (1971), is much more accurate about history (though one wonders how De Sica would have fared had he extended the Finzi Continis family saga to encompass Auschwitz).

Benigni is not the only recent Italian film maker to treat the war years in this near romantic fashion. In Franco Zeffirelli's "Tea with Mussolini" (1999), the reality of the Fascist terror—the deportations, the brutality of the police and military—are

---

[6]Jon Hoberman, "Dreaming the Unthinkable," <u>Sight and Sound</u> (February, 1999).

glossed over. In this "soothing, deeply sentimental, old-fashioned memory piece," viewers are not allowed to get distracted by horror as they root for the "scorpioni," a group of resourceful British and American women in war-torn Florence[7]. In the end, like Benigni's endearing Guido, these sprightly women (played by Judi Dench, Joan Plowright, Maggie Smith, and Lili Tomlin) manage to beat the Nazi system as well. In the process, they make us feel good about the amazing power of courage and the human spirit. Their efforts to smuggle out of Italy a Jewish woman (Cher), who befriends the ladies, is, no doubt, their most remarkable accomplishment. She is a rich American, a patron of the arts, an eccentric woman patterned on the legendary Peggy Guggenheim. Her escape is smooth and painless: no blood, no killings, just a clean exit through Switzerland.

"Train of Life," a film completed before "Life is Beautiful" but only released in America a year after the Italian film, is much less problematic than Benigni's creation. As Mihaileanu's Jews are shown neither in ghettoes nor in concentration camps, he did not have to deal with issues of realism when shooting such scenes, a task that has bedeviled every visual artist trying to recreate the Shoah experience. The first half of Mihaileanu's film takes place in a small Romanian village, a typical Eastern European shtetl, an easy location as most of these towns have not changed much since the war. The second half unfolds on the "train of life," a fake cattle-car train heading East toward Russia, and to freedom from Nazi-occupied territory. In both films, the hero who triumphs over evil is a village fool, a comical character with the right instincts and the right ploys to trick the Nazis. Benigni's clown is shown as a very lucky fellow; Shloyme, the village fool in "Train of Life," seems to be inspired from above, as if through him divine intervention saves the day whenever

---

[7]National Review (June 28, 1999).

the Jews are about to fall into the hands of the Nazis.

The crucial difference is that Mihaileanu's work is free of ambiguities and manipulation of historical facts. "Train of Life" is an honest film about a fantasy, a brilliant idea of how the Shoah, at least for this shtetl, could have been avoided. "Life is Beautiful," with its muted Jewishness, ambiguous settings and characters, is so concerned with universalizing the events that we forget that we are in the midst of the Shoah and the victims are Jews.

With regards to comedy and the Shoah, Robert Sklar's assessment is correct: these films ("Train of Life," "Jacob the Liar," "Life is Beautiful") "regard comic resistance as a form of moral triumph."[8] I, too, detect a trend developing—events being used as moral lessons, as ideal vehicles for producing uplifting messages about the human spirit. I suggested earlier that even if we accept the premise of Benigni's film—its fable-like atmosphere, the parody, the games—comedy should not be construed as licence for violating history, an excuse for painting a false, albeit entertaining, picture of the events. Mihaileanu, on the other hand, has shown that comedy and history could be compatible, even if the story is as fantastic as "The Wizard of Oz."

While "Life is Beautiful," "Tea with Mussolini" and "Train of Life" are set in distant Europe, "Apt Pupil" and "The Devil's Arithmetic" deal with the Shoah in an American context. Bryan Singer's "Apt Pupil" is based on Stephen King's "Needful Things," a horrifying tale of evil and moral corruption in a provincial Midwestern town. Todd (Brad Renfro) is a typical all-American A student at the local highschool. A class on the Holocaust inspires him to set off on a mission to

---

[8]Robert Sklar, "Looking at the Escapist Impulses Behind the New Holocaust Cinema," Forward (November 5, 1999).

find out if a man riding on the bus, a man who resembles a picture of a Nazi officer he saw in a book, are indeed one and the same person. It turns out this man is Kurt Dussander (Ian McKellen), a former concentration camp officer with a great deal of information on how those terrible things he read about in history books, were actually carried out.

Todd's morbid fascination with the former Nazi leads to a series of disturbing changes in him: his grades are sliding, he loses interest in girls, and performs poorly on the basketball court. Worst of all, however, is Todd's metamorphosis from an honest, decent young man, to a deceitful immoral person. A few weeks in Dussander's shadow and Todd feels no compunction about cheating, lying, even killing a homeless man who accidentally wanders into Dussander's home.

The film is vintage Stephen King: an isolated, spooky house, a mysterious man with a dark past, an impressionable young student who falls under his spell. And of course, there is murder, nightmares and gruesome deaths. Around this, director Bryan Singer narrates a bizarre tale of evil and corruption. Todd's experience seems to teach us a moral lesson: no one is safe around evil of this sort; when even the most upright among us can be ruined, when a boy like Todd is capable of committing unspeakable acts, should anyone be surprised at the Germans under Nazism? Are not the Germans people like us, who were once decent and good, but got corrupted by evil? They were not monsters, they were not aberrant; like Todd, they simply fell under the spell of the deadly, irresistible virus called immorality. Once free of any social constraints (political, judicial, religious), the Nazis set off on one of history's bloodiest rampages, creating a nightmare that Dostoevsky almost a century earlier had warned could befall us if we were not careful enough.

It appears that the students who committed the cold-blooded murders in the Spring of 1999 at Columbine High School in Colorado somehow managed to enter that dangerous zone of moral void—of total indifference toward human life—even without a Nazi mass murderer as mentor. Does "Apt Pupil" suggest that getting too close to evil can infect us so badly that we might become the very evil we are trying to expunge? Is this dark evil, this "Heart of Darkness," so overpowering that we better avoid it unless we are willing to pay the consequences? Is the Shoah just another example of evil left unchecked, a product of sadists like Dussander running amok, fulfilling every bit of twisted fantasy in the morally hollow jungle of Nazi Germany? While all this is interesting, missing from this picture are two millennia of anti-Semitism, history, politics and economics, all essential factors in understanding the roots of this, the twentieth century's worst human catastrophe.

In this horror film, which is stripped of historicity and particularity, it was important that Todd not be Jewish, thus removing any personal motives from his obsession with the Shoah. He is drawn to it, not necessarily because Jews were murdered but because of the fascination with what struck him as evil incarnate, the highest form of cruelty man ever perpetrated toward another human being.

Hannah, another highschool student, the main hero in "The Devil's Arithmetic," is a typical assimilated suburban Jew from New Rochelle, New York. Unlike Todd who learns about it in school, she lives with it at every family gathering and on holidays when invariably aunts and uncles, Holocaust survivors, reminisce about their past in Europe. Like typical American teenagers, she prefers the movies or shopping to listening to depressing stories of suffering and death.

Her attitude toward the Shoah and Judaism is the reason she is miraculously transported back in time from New Rochelle to the shtetl in Poland where her relatives had lived before the war. Once there, Hannah learns a great deal about religion and traditions as practiced in Eastern Europe, and eventually experiences the ordeals of deportation and life in a concentration camp. But unlike her friends and relatives (her parents, as a Polish girl, are dead), many of whom die in the camps, Hannah knows she will survive because she knows the future. In fact, some of the film's most touching moments occur when she tells her friends and relatives what will happen to them and their families. In the midst of gloom, however, several amusing scenes stand out: the typical 1990s American girl explaining to her 1940s Polish peers the meaning of shopping malls, pizza and hamburgers!

The novel, upon which the film is based, was written for teenagers and is used in Holocaust education classes. Placing a teenager at the center is intended to increase the book's appeal among this highly problematic age group. In addition to raising interest in the Shoah, the novel is also promoting Jewish tradition. (Hannah's voyage to the past occurs over a Passover Seder as she yawns away the evening.) These are clearly noble aspirations and one hopes they are achieved with every reading or viewing.

In its cinematic incarnation, however, "The Devil's Arithmetic" (produced by Dustin Hoffman) offers a rather skewed view of shtetl life in Poland. All Jews are religious, they all live happily with each other until the Germans arrive in town totally unexpected, literally in the middle of a Rabbi's son's wedding! Shots of the village—an actual town outside Vilna—only show Jews, as if this were an urban ghetto. All this, of course, is incorrect since shtetl Jews lived among Gentiles. Even more inaccurate is the depiction of the concentration camp. It is too obvious that this unnamed camp was neatly put together with prefabricated material; things appear too artificial, too reminiscent of the sets in the NBC TV series, "Holocaust," where it was clear that everything we saw was poorly improvised. Camps were not built in wide open fields in the middle of nowhere, and men and women were not able to see or talk to each other as easily as it is shown here. Also, showing Germans as caricatures—barking orders, speaking with funny German accents, does not produce the desired effect. As readers of Primo Levi and Elie Wiesel know only too well, only rarely did prisoners come into contact with the Germans since the dirty work was left to the kapos and Ukrainian or Lithuanian guards.[9] Prisoners in "The Devil's Arithmetic" are too fat, too healthy-looking; most amazingly, they manage to produce a Seder that includes the use of a wood stove!

I am wondering if the idea of punishing someone like Hannah for not honoring tradition and the memory of the Holocaust is appropriate. Does it have any impact on young readers or viewers? I suspect that many are horrified, even put off by it. These problems notwithstanding, the two young women in the film, Kirsten Dunst as Hannah and Brittany Murphy as her cousin Rivka, play their parts with great skill and feeling. A few bright spots, however, do not save the film from failure; this youth-oriented work ignores the fact that today's teenagers are sophisticated viewers who do not tolerate fake-looking sets, historical inaccuracies and improbable plots, unless they understand that what they are watching is fantasy or fairy tale .

It is to the credit of the producers of "Jacob the Liar" that this film was made to look authentic. Since the opening of Eastern Europe following the fall of Communism, many films about pre-war Jews are now being shot on location, including the ghetto scenes used here. Though not explicit about it, everything points to Lodz, a large city in Eastern Poland, close to the Russian border. The year is 1944, late in the war, and the Allies are making progress on several fronts. But the Jews within the ghetto walls have no way of finding out what goes on in the outside world. Jacob (Robin Williams) wanders into the German headquarters by mistake and listens to a news broadcast about the fighting on the Russian front. This gives him

---

[9]Levi wrote a great deal about the lager (concentration camp) hierarchy in his memoirs, Survival in Auschwitz, trans. Stuart Woolf (New York: Collier Books, 1993), and The Drowned and the Saved, trans. Raymond Rosenthal (New York: Summit Books, 1988).

the idea of pretending that he has a secret radio and he starts spreading cheering stories in the news-starved ghetto.

When faced with the dilemma of continuing this pretense and risking increased German danger, or telling the truth, Jacob is persuaded by the ghetto's Jewish doctor (Armin Muller-Stahl, who starred in the original, 1974 German version as well) to continue with it, as the good news helps boost the morale which in turn increases the survival rate. In the end, the Germans arrest and hang him in a public square because he doesn't produce the mysterious radio. As with "Life is Beautiful," we are once again expected to accept fiction posing as historical fact: in "Jacob the Liar" we are expected to believe that the film's central premise—radios were the only way to get news—is actually what happened in the ghettoes. Nothing could be further from the truth: news filtered through via smuggled newspapers, workers from the outside, and a variety of underground channels of information.

The director of this film tries very hard to weave a number of loosely connected incidents into Jacob's story, but as Stanley Kaufmann correctly observes, "that's really all there is to the story (the radio ruse)."[10] Though completed before "Life is Beautiful," "Jacob the Liar," starring America's leading clown, Robin Williams, will always be judged in terms of the work of that other popular clown—arguably Europe's best—Roberto Benigni. In Benigni's film, the main hero triumphs over evil and darkness through clever schemes; in Kassovitz's film, the latke peddler is equally resourceful in his own battles with the Nazis. Their death at the end shows that one can push his luck only so far before meeting destiny. Both schemes involve some very moving acts—in "Life is Beautiful" the father saves his son, in "Jacob the Liar" Jacob saves a young girl. In Benigni's film, however, the personal story is

---

[10]Stanley Kaufmann, "Fantasy Peddlers," The New Republic (October 25, 1999).

engaging throughout; in Kassovitz's "Jacob the Liar" the drama of Jacob, the Germans, and the deluded Jews, is too drawn out, ultimately becoming too tedious to keep us interested.

The two works share one other important element though: they both strip the material of its Jewish content. As noted, Benigni, contrary to many public statements, uses the Shoah as a metaphor, a backdrop to a fundamentally universal tale of humor and humanity triumphing over evil; Jurek Becker's book and Kassovitz's film version are about hope as an effective antidote to despair and death. While slightly more Jewish than the Italian film, "Jacob the Liar" is not very generous on ethnicity. The only Jewishness here is Jacob blurting out an occasional Yiddish word, the Yellow Star on coats, and a soundtrack that uses motifs of klezmer music. Missing from Kassovitz's ghetto universe is the intense religious, cultural and social life of these doomed prisoners who defied the enemy and imminent death by desperately trying to act as "normal" as possible.[11]

In the end, unlike "Life is Beautiful," "Jacob the Liar" fails because it has a weak plot. Having a great cast and a great location do not guarantee success; to succeed, a Shoah film needs gripping drama, preferably the kind found in "Sophie's Choice" and "Schindler's List." This is not to say that even these popular films are without some flaws: as I argued in my previous essay on the Shoah, the plots of these

---

[11] The ghetto experience is treated in history books on the Shoah. The greatest literary tribute to the incredible cultural vitality inside these giant urban prisons is Joshua Sobol's internationally acclaimed play, "Ghetto." Published in Hebrew in 1983, the play appeared on various European and American stages. It has also been translated into a dozen languages including Dutch, Finnish, and Polish. Ghetto (Tel Aviv: Or Am, 1983); Ghetto, David Lan trans. (London: Nick Hern Books, 1989).

In America, the best known work on the subject is Leslie Epstein's King of the Jews, (New York: Summit Books, 1979), a novel about Haim Rumkovsky, the controversial head of the Lodz ghetto. Isaiah Trunk's monumental work, Judenrat (New York: McMillan, 1972), is the most extensive study of ghetto life and politics.

box office hits do not tell the typical Shoah story: what is viewed is far from what happened to the large majority of victims. Nonetheless, as I also argued, even these highly sensationalist versions of the Holocaust are valuable educational tools since they help preserve the memory of the Shoah, trigger public debates, and even enlighten those in the dark about the events. Unfortunately, "Jacob the Liar" has only caused a small ripple before quickly vanishing from the screen. Hopefully, in video form, the film will be seen by more people despite its weaknesses, as "Jacob the Liar" does introduce the public to an often misunderstood or ignored aspect of the Shoah, namely the ghetto experience.

"Apt Pupil," the only film covered in this essay that is not set in the Shoah proper, is free of the pitfalls facing films that are set in the war proper, either in ghettoes or camps. Still, "Apt Pupil" fails because the Shoah does not lend itself to Stephen King and horror-movie genre treatment. Even a great actor like Ian McKullen could not save it from its sad fate; in the end, the Shoah, the Jews, the former Nazi, are all obscured by stylistic maneuvers and implausible incidents—a former Nazi living alone in a big house, a young boy doing FBI-type work to track him down, etc., etc. In "Life is Beautiful" and "The Devil's Arithmetic," on the other hand, part of the action unfolds in concentration camps; even if we accept the premise of these films' plots, these are flawed works as the war scenes look too much like sets, not at all real. The same applies to the prisoners and the guards. Understandably, creating realistic depictions of concentration camps, the prisoners and the guards is a daunting task, perhaps an impossible one, but if one chooses realism it must look like the "real thing" or it loses credibility. I believe viewers are more tolerant of neutral sets with minimal props, perhaps something more in keeping with Beckett and "Theater of the Absurd" than the transparently fake images present in these films.

What emerges from these and the works discussed in the previous Shoah essay is that great drama tends to be atypical or it drowns the events in the personal ("Sophie's Choice," "Schindler's List," "Europa, Europa"); thin plots, though set in great locations with authentic-looking characters, fail to attract audiences ("Jacob the Liar"); despite their noble motives, films with highly contrived plots and shabby sets ("The Devil's Arithmetic"), are ineffective; good plots treated in an inappropriate way ("Apt Pupil") fail as well. An excellent film like the "Train of Life" is relegated to the foreign, "artsy" film category which limits its exposure significantly.

In the end, the only films that can totally satisfy are documentaries. But documentaries have little or no entertainment value, drawing on very limited audiences, usually the kind found in academic settings or professional conferences. Naturally, crowds will rush to see the next "Schindler's List," but only a fraction will go to see the next nine-hour marathon of Lanzmann's "Shoah." There are no easy solutions to this thorny problem. But as long as the viewing public prefers the fiction feature film over the non-fiction one, film makers must make films that show respect for history and the memory of the victims.

Jewish Wedding Bells: Hollywood 2000 Style

Lately, movies seemed to have embraced the age-old institution of marriage like never before. We need only think of such recent blockbusters as "The Wedding Banquet," "Monsoon Wedding," "My Big Fat Greek Wedding" and "Late Marriage" to get an idea of the extent of this cultural phenomenon. According to Lori Leibovich, one database shows that there are 350 films, television movies and videos with the word "wedding" in the title. She also points out that "our seemingly insatiable appetite for these schmaltzy, predictable wedding comedies results from the way they feed our sentimental attachment to love and marriage while simultaneously undercutting it with humor."[1] Since all the cinematic weddings I cite involve a particular ethnic or national group (Chinese, Indian, Greek, Israeli-Georgian), the main conflict usually revolves around the "right" or "wrong" choices that the heroes make. In all cases, the younger generation is at odds with the parents over the background of the mates. Nowhere is this truer than in "Greek Wedding" as viewers cheered for the marriage-bound couple—Toula Portokalos, the very ethnic Greek woman, and Ian Miller, the extremely waspy young man—to resolve their problems.

As far as recent American films are concerned, we find that Jewish weddings play a key role in Hollywood's preoccupation with ethnic identity and politics. Three works stand out: "Keeping the Faith" (Edward Norton, 2000); "What's Cooking?" (Gurinder Chadha, 2000); and "Kissing Jessica Stein" (Charles Herman-Wurmfeld, 2002). As we shall see, like other ethnic-centered works, these three films also present the conflict between the young and old over problematic unions (usually mixed marriages), but in the end, compromise and compassion prevail. Religion is

---

[1] Lori Leibovich, "The Fail-Safe Summer Wedding Films," The New York Times (May 10, 2003).

important, but only up to a point.

"Keeping the Faith" presents a very entertaining dilemma: can a pair of New York friends—a young rabbi (Ben Stiller) and a young priest (Edward Norton)—figure out who gets the girl of his dreams? Of course, she is verboten to both, to the rabbi because she is not Jewish, and to the priest because of his vows of celibacy. But, to understand things, we must go back a few years. As teenagers, Jake (the rabbi), Brian (the priest) and Anna were best friends. But after high school, Anna's family moved to California and the two boys lost all contact with the girl. Back to the present—Anna (Jenna Elfman of "Dharma and Greg"), now a stunning blonde, returns to New York as a powerful corporate executive. Jake and Brian fall immediately in love. Jake is a junior rabbi at an Upper West Side synagogue where he is carefully groomed to take over the reins of the congregation from a retiring leader, his father. Among others, Jake is pressured by all, including his very determined parents (played by the ever-popular showbiz "Jewish" couple of Eli Wallach and Anne Bancroft), to find a suitable mate and settle down.

In principle, an unmarried rabbi could lead the flock, but that is a rare thing. Under pressure to settle down, Jake embarks on a series of arranged dates with, of course, "nice Jewish girls," among them, Rachel, the television reporter, who is much more focused on herself and a promising career than on relationships (she is all excited about an upcoming interview with Saddam Hussein—in Arabic, no less!), and Chaya, an overly aggressive, flaky girl who wants to have sex the first night out. Clearly, no one measures up to Anna's beauty, charm and, above all, her irresistible nature, especially since she is strictly verboten by dint of her religion. As expected, Jake's parents are pretty shaken by the news; another son had also fallen in love with a *shikse*, married her, and moved to California. His father has not spoken to him ever since. In Jake's case, the mother is equally forgiving. The father, on the other hand, is adamant about his feelings on this crucial issue: his son, the new head rabbi, is not going to marry a gentile!

About to be relocated to San Francisco, Anna tells Jake that she loves him. However, he refuses to commit, and they temporarily break up. Then, in a final act of desperation, he announces to a stunned congregation that he is in love with a Gentile woman and plans to marry her. His liberal flock forgives him, and after some debate, the leaders of the congregation approve his candidacy as new rabbi. He rushes to tell Anna, and to his great surprise, he learns that, secretly, she has been preparing for this very moment by taking conversion classes with his father, the elder rabbi. His fiend Brian, the young priest, is left to drown his sorrows at losing the girl in a series of whisky shots at a bar tended by an Indian man who is the true incarnation of multiculturalism: he is, as he confesses, "half-Punjabi, Sikh Catholic Muslim with Jewish in-laws."

Religion in "Keeping the Faith" seems to be practiced very differently and by two kinds of people: the older generation, represented by Jake's father and the synagogue board of directors, and the younger practitioners like Jake and his Catholic friend. While most of the old timers try desperately to cling to traditions and customs, the younger people are bent on changing things radically. As most of us remember, in the old days clerics were vastly different from their flock; but, as David Denby points out in Norton's film, "under their cloth, these two clerics are regular guys . . . they wear shades and leather jackets, digging the city, bantering each other . . . while each has a calling, a gift."[2] As hip, young men of cloth, the two preach an extreme liberal brand of religious openness to all people, tolerance of personal failings, embrace of "the other" whether that be a gay person, an atheist or, as with

---

[2] David Denby, The New Yorker (April 24, 2000).

Jake and Anna, approval of a matrimonial union between Jew and Gentile.

This eventual union is emblematic of a wider phenomenon. Not only are Jake and Anna united, but through their travails whole communities of previously divided groups are brought together in a show of brotherhood and harmony. As the final scene is about to fade, a group of adults at a city social club are seen dancing—Jews with Gentiles, blacks with whites, wasps with Hispanics—a veritable tableau of an American paradise that Martin Luther King could only dream of. As a utopian picture it is very refreshing and inspiring. As a mirror of reality it could not be any further from the truth. While religious and ethnic groups coexist rather peacefully in New York (by extension, the entire northeast), they have little to do with each other: Jewish centers cater to Jews, Churches to Christians, etc. Usually, mixed couples tend to either discard religion or if they do decide to practice anything, it is the religion of one of the converted partners.

Like Jake, Jessica Stein (Jennifer Westfeld), the main hero of "Kissing Jessica Stein," is also struggling to find the right mate in Manhattan's confusing and complex jungle of single partners. Her journey takes her to dates with drug addicts, "dorky accountants," macho self-centered jerks, etc. Jessica works as a copy editor for a hip downtown magazine; her coworkers are the usual assortment of bisexuals as well as some gays and lesbians. Jessica's home is in Scarsdale, where her overbearing mother (the great Tovah Feldshuh) is pushing her to find a "nice Jewish boy" and settle down. Jessica's older brother is engaged and is soon to be married to a "nice Jewish girl."

One particular personal ad catches Jessica's eye; upon meeting the author of the ad, Jessica finds Helen to be a successful, sexy young woman who runs a downtown art gallery and is also seeking "the right mate" (in her case, a lesbian). After some initial discomfort and confusion, Jessica makes up her mind: she will give this a try. She has never been with a woman. She will, somehow, break the news to her caring mother in suburban Scarsdale where such liaisons are very rare and, if they do exist, kept secret, unlike in SoHo. Ironically, all this is happening while wedding preparations for Jessica's brother are in full swing. As invitations are printed, family and friends anticipated, dresses fitted, flowers ordered, and halls booked, Jessica has to decide how to introduce Helen to the family. Sensing her daughter's torment, Mrs. Judy Stein reassures Jessica that she understands and approves of the relationship; she is welcome to bring along Helen to the wedding party. As Erin Gill points out, this is "a poignant but unsentimental moment when Judy acknowledges that her daughter is in love with a woman."[3]

Mrs. Stein is not a religious woman. She lives alone in a beautiful house. She keeps what could be described as an "ethnic" home where Shabbes and major holidays are marked with candle-lighting ceremonies, a trip to the temple, and, of course, festive dinners.

It is precisely at the dinner, arranged in honor of the groom, where Jessica experiences a change of direction. One of the invited guests is Josh, Jessica's supervisor at the magazine, an old college friend, who is also a friend of the groom, Jessica's brother. Josh is a single heterosexual Jew, who treats Jessica with a mixture of respect, affection and a certain degree of brotherly love. Being with her in a private setting away from office work and official functions offers an opportunity to sort out feelings a little better. While Helen is still in the picture, the two realize that they have more than just a college past and the present workplace in common; in fact, they feel rather close and ready to embark on something romantic and long lasting. Religion is not mentioned. In the end, what had to be cleared was Jessica's sexuality

---

[3]Erin Gill, <u>Film Journal International</u>, Spring 2002.

and not her misgivings about being with or marrying a Gentile, which is what Helen is. As one reviewer put it, "One is the Jewish American Princess, the other the daft artnik with the killer body; but in time, you don't see Jewish and cute or gentile and hot, you just see people."[4] Following several more twists and turns, Jessica and Josh come together and seem to be clearly headed towards commitment and marriage.

Interestingly, both, Jake and Jessica had to travel the frustrating and bumpy road of serial dating before arriving at the one person from their past that lay there waiting for that proverbial "magical moment" of two fond hearts eventually coming together in love. For Jake it was Anna, his childhood sweetheart; for Jessica it was Josh, her college friend. In the first case, the young rabbi ends up marrying the beautiful *shikse* after a series of disappointing Jewish dates; however, this *shikse* becomes a Jew herself, silencing any Jewish critics who might object to this union. In "Kissing Jessica Stein," Jessica Stein will indeed marry the Jewish man after being with a string of odd eligible men and one irresistible but problematic mate—the hip, experienced, vivacious "downtown Helen." In the end, the "right choice" involves serious religious and sexual tribulations. Differences aside, in both films the Jewish character ultimately marries a Jew, either by birth or by conversion.

This is not the case in "What's Cooking?," the 2000 multicultural comedy directed by Gurinder Chadha, a Kenya-born Englishwoman of Indian descent. Shot around that all-American holiday Thanksgiving, the film focuses on four Los Angeles families about to cut the turkey. They are Hispanic, African-American, Jewish and Vietnamese. Thanksgiving was the perfect choice, for as Roger Ebert correctly observes, this holiday "is not hooked to any national or ethnic group . . . we exchange no presents and send few cards. It's on a Thursday, a day not associated with any

---

[4]Stephen Hunter, The Washington Post (March 20, 2002).

belief system. And it nods gratefully to American Indians who have good reason to feel less than thrilled about the Fourth of July and Columbus Day.[5]

As the respective meals are being carefully and lovingly prepared, we learn of each family's crisis. At the Avila household, the always-enchanting Mercedes Ruehl plays the divorced mother about to present to her entire clan her new mate, a white colleague she met at the school where she teaches. Complications arise when, unbeknownst to her, her son invites the father to celebrate with the family. What could be spicier than a hot-blooded Latino ex-husband and a lover at the same table?

The Williams couple are well-to-do professionals. First, they have to cope with an overbearing mother just arrived from Chicago, second, an absent college boy who seems to be much happier working for a variety of social and political causes than studying. His activism is a source of embarrassment for the father, who is employed by none other than the controversial right-wing, white governor of California. Finally, the Williams couple has some serious marital issues that need to be resolved; otherwise, they are surely headed for disaster.

The Nguyens are proprietors of a video rental store. They too seem to have lost control of their children's lives. The parents, who were born "over there" do not have a clue what goes on in their two teenage children's American lives. While luckily nothing serious happens, these very old-fashioned parents are stunned to find an unopened condom under the daughter's bed, and shocked to learn that their son may be connected with some street gang in the neighborhood.

Before touching on the Seligs, the Jewish family in the mix, it would be worth quoting Kevin Thomas's remarks about this work. He writes: "The film seesaws between tradition and change with its people learning as they go what's important to

---

[5]Roger Ebert, Chicago-Sun Times (November 12, 2000).

hold onto and let go of. As a result, "What's Cooking?" captures the spirit of family life in contemporary Los Angeles to a degree unexpected in a mainstream movie."[6]

"What's important to hold onto and let go of" captures so well the dilemma facing the Jewish family in "What's Cooking?" The mother (played by the indestructible Lainie Kazan) and the father are a pair of retired Jews living in a typical Los Angeles multi-ethnic neighborhood. They are eagerly awaiting the arrival of Rachel, their only daughter (played by the very talented Kyra Sedwick), a successful young woman living for years with another woman, Carla (played by another extremely gifted actress, Julianna Margulies). Like Mrs. Stein, these Jewish parents have to decide whether to continue insisting that their precious children conform to their traditional views of family, or to "let go of" and accept the younger ones' choices, even if those choices are difficult, even impossible to comprehend.

Thus, Rachel is very careful not to insult her parents by being overtly affectionate towards her friend while at the same time trying to make Carla feel welcome in the house in which she grew up. In fact, in a twist of irony, the young women wind up sleeping—at first in separate beds—in Rachel's old bedroom! The parents, for their part, use this rare visit to occasionally remind their daughter of the joys of parenthood as well as grandparenthood; in their case provided by the two twins born to Rachel's married brother, who also happens to live nearby. (No matter that when the happy family arrives, all hell breaks loose and the blessed grandparents cannot wait for the little devils to depart.) Despite the festive occasion, the overall atmosphere in the Selig household is rather tense as the two women try desperately to avoid touching or doing anything that would give away their true feelings. While the parents are fully aware, the guests, at first, are not.

---

[6]Kevin Thomas, <u>Los Angeles Times</u> (November 17, 2000).

No one, including the parents, was prepared for the bomb that falls right in the middle of the turkey dinner: Rachel announces to the stunned family and friends that she and Carla are going to have a baby with Rachel as the recipient of artificial insemination! All that an old aunt can mutter is, "But is the baby going to be Jewish?" So, while no Jewish wedding is in the offing, the Seligs may comfort themselves with the thought that their dear daughter is soon going to give them more grandchildren. It is not clear what it is more difficult for the Seligs to digest, the fact that their child is a homosexual or the birth of a child through artificial means. In any event, like all good parents, the Seligs love their daughter no matter what. They seem reconciled to the fact that one child has followed the traditional path, while the other—clearly the darling of both parents—has strayed a bit. As expected, when confronted with such a major problem as same sex marriage, the religious issues are marginal. In fact, we do not know whether Carla is Jewish.

This situation brings to mind "Chutney Popcorn" (`Nisha Ganatra, 2000), a film about Indian families living in England. Set in present-day Britain, Reena is an open lesbian; her sister Sarita is married but, because of some rare medical condition, cannot carry to term. A solution is found when Reena agrees to be inseminated by Sarita's husband and get pregnant in her sister's place. The sisters' mother, a much more traditional person than Mrs. Selig, finds the whole business disgusting and threatens to punish, even disown Reena. But, like the Seligs, she too comes around to accepting her children's unconventional choices.

In "Keeping the Faith," the sexy *shikse* eventually converts, and all is fine in Jewland. In "Kissing Jessica Stein," the young eligible woman eventually comes to her senses and is about to marry the nice Jewish boy she knew from college. In "What's Cooking?" things are more complex. Here, Jews are seen as simply one piece of the puzzle. Young Latinos and Asians are seen mixing freely with other groups, so why not Jews? In this case, the other group happens to be gay. Of course, the issue with the Seligs is procreation and the Jewish preoccupation with perpetuating the race. But, as director Chadha shows, even that can be resolved through artificial insemination. In the end, parents in all ethnic groups shown here, are usually more conservative, but they come around to accepting their children's choices; after all, it was they (the parents or grandparents) who chose to live in America and not in some other, more traditional place. If "What's Cooking?" is an indicator, as a piece of this fascinating ethnic/religious/racial tapestry, Jews are faced with the same dilemma others face every day in this fast-moving, ultra-modern society—"what to hold onto, and what to let go of?"

APPENDIX

Select Bibliography and Filmography

Film History and Criticism

Avisar, Ilan. *Screening the Holocaust: Cinema's Images of the Unimaginable*. Bloomington: Indiana University Press, 1988.
Bernheimer, Kathryn. *The 50 Greatest Jewish Movies*. Secaucus, NJ: Carol Publishing Group, 1998.
Cohen, Sarah Blacher (ed.). *From Hester Street to Hollywood: The Jewish-American Stage and Screen*. Bloomington: Indiana University Press, 1983.
Doneson, Judith. *The Holocaust in American Film*. Philadelphia: Jewish Publication Society, 1987.
Erens, Patricia. *The Jew in American Cinema*. Bloomington: Indiana University Press, 1984.
Friedman, Lester. *Hollywood's Image of the Jew*. New York: Ungar Publishing Co., 1982.
Friedman, Lester and David Desser. *American-Jewish Filmmakers: Traditions and Trends*. Urbana: University of Illinois Press, 1993.
Gabler, Neal. *An Empire of their Own: How the Jews Invented Hollywood*. New York, 1988.
Hoberman, Jon. *Bridge of Light: Yiddish Film Between Two Worlds*. Philadelphia: Temple University Press, 1995.
Insdorf, Annette. *Indelible Shadows: Film and the Holocaust*. Cambridge: Cambridge University Press, 1983.
Kronish, Amy. *World Cinema: Israel*. Cranbury, NJ: Associated University Press, 1996.
Shohat, Ella. *Israeli Cinema: East/West and the Politics of Representation*. Austin: University of Texas Press, 1989.
Schnitzer, Meir. *Hakolnoa Haisraeli (Israeli Cinema)*. Jerusalem: Kinneret, 1994.

Jewish-American History

Dinnerstein, Leonard. *Uneasy at Home: Antisemitism and the American Jewish Experience.* New York: Columbia University Press, 1987.
Feingold, Henry. *A Time for Searching: Entering the Mainstream, 1920-1945.* Baltimore: Johns Hopkins University Press, 1992.
Glazer, Nathan. *American Judaism.* Chicago, 1957.
Hentoff, Nat (ed.). *Black Antisemitism and Jewish Racism.* New York, 1969.
Hertzberg, Arthur. *The Jews in America: Four Centuries of an Uneasy Encounter.* New York: Simon and Schuster, 1989.
Hertzberg, Arthur. *Being Jewish in America: The Modern Experience.* New York: Schocken Books, 1979.
Howe, Irving. *World of Our Fathers.* New York: Schocken Books, 1976.
Moore, Deborah Dash and Paula Heyman. *Jewish Women in America.* New York: Routledge, 1997.
Sklare, Marshall (ed.). *The Jews: Social Patterns of an American Group.* Glencoe, IL, 1959.

Holocaust History

Bauer, Yehuda. *A History of the Holocaust.* New York: Franklin Watts, 1982.
Dawidowicz, Lucy. *The War Against the Jews.* New York: Bantam Books, 1981.
Dwork, Deborah and Robert Jan van Pelt. *Holocaust: A History.* New York: W. W. Norton and Co., 2002.
Hilberg, Raul. *The Destruction of the European Jewry.* New York: Harper&Row, 1961.
Katz, Steven. *The Holocaust in Historical Context.* New York: Oxford University Press, 1994.
Levin, Nora. *The Holocaust: The Destruction of European Jewry, 1933-1945.* New York: Thomas Crowell Company, 1968.
Marrus, Michael. *The Holocaust in History.* Hanover, NH: University Press of New England, 1987.
Yahil, Leni. *The Holocaust.* New York: Oxford University Press, 1990.

Israel

Elon, Amos. *The Israelis: Founders and Sons*. New York: Penguin Books, 1981.
Sachar, Howard. *A History of Israel: From the Rise of Zionism to Our Time*. New York: Knopf, 1985.
Taub, Michael (ed.). *An Anthology of Israeli Drama for the New Millennium*. Lewiston, NY: The Edwin Mellen Press, 2004.

Fiction Feature Films and Some Documentaries

This is not a comprehensive list. These works were chosen because they deal with Jewish issues in a significant manner. Another criteria is that they are familiar to the English-speaking audience.

Aimee and Jaguar (Germany, Max Farberbock, 1998)
Almost Peaceful (France, Michel Deville, 2002)
Amen (France, Costa-Gavras, 2001)
Annie Hall (USA, Woody Allen, 1977)
The Apprenticeship of Duddy Kravitz (USA, Ted Kotcheff, 1974)
Apt Pupil (USA, Bryan Singer, 1999)
Ashes and Diamonds (Poland, Andrzej Wajda, 1958)
Au Revoir Les Enfants (France, Louis Malle, 1987)
Autumn Sun (Argentina, Eduardo Mignogna, 1996)
Avalon (USA, Barry Levinson, 1990)
Avanti Popolo (Israel, Rafi Bukai, 1986)
The Believer (USA, Henry Bean, 2001)
Benya Krik (USSR, V. Vilner, 1926)
Blazing Saddles (USA, Mel Brooks, 1974)
Blind Man's Bluff (Israel, Anat Preminger, 1992)
The Boat Is Full (Switzerland-Germany-Austria, Markus Imhoof, 1981)
Brighton Beach Memoirs (USA, Gene Saks, 1986)
Broken Glass (BBC Production, David Thacker, 1996)
Cast A Giant Shadow (USA, Melville Shavelson, 1966)
Chariots of Fire (UK, Hugh Hudson, 1981)
The Chosen (USA, Jeremy P. Kagan, 1982)
Chicks in White Stain (USA, Elaine Holliman, 1993)
Commissar (USSR, Alexander Askoldov, 1967)
Crossing Delancey (USA, Joan M. Silver, 1988)
Daniel (USA, Sidney Lumet, 1983)

David (Germany, Peter Lilienthal, 1979)
The Devil's Arithmetic (USA, Donna Deitch, 1999)
Deconstructing Harry (USA, Woody Allen, 1997)
Diamonds of the Night (Czech, Jan Nemec, 1964)
The Diary of Anne Frank (USA, George Stevens, 1959)
Dogs: The Rise and Fall of an All Girl Bookie Joint (USA, Eve Annenberg, 1996)
Driving Miss Daisy (USA, Bruce Beresford, 1989)
The Dybbuk (Poland, M. Waszynski, 1937)
Enemies, A Love Story (USA, Paul Mazursky, 1989)
Entre Nous (France, Diane Kurys, 1983)
Europa, Europa (French-German, Agnieszka Holland, 1991)
Exodus (USA, Otto Preminger, 1960)
Fiddler on the Roof (USA, Norman Jewison, 1971)
The Frisco Kid (USA, Robert Aldrich, 1979)
The Garden of the Finzi-Continis (Italy, Vittorio De Sica, 1970)
Gentleman's Agreement (USA, Elia Kazan, 1947)
Goodbye, Columbus (USA, Larry Peerce, 1969)
Goodbye New York (Israel, Amos Kolek, 1984)
The Governess (UK, Sandra Goldbacher, 1998)
Green Fields (Poland, Edgar Ulmer and Jacob Ben Ami, 1937)
Hamsin (Israel, Daniel Wachsmann, 1983)
Hanna's War (USA, Menachem Golan, 1988)
The Harmonists (Germany, Joseph Vilsmaier, 1998)
From Hell to Hell (Germany, Dimitry Astrakhan, 1997)
Hester Street (USA, Joan M. Silver, 1975)
Hitchhikers (Israel, Dudu Topaz, 1998)
Holocaust (NBC-TV, Marvin Chomsky, 1978)
The House on Cheloushe Street (Israel, M. Golan, 1973)
The Island on Bird Street ("Showtime," TV, 1998)
Jacob the Liar (USA, Peter Kassovitz, 1999)
Jacob der Lugner (East Germany, Frank Beyer, 1978)
The Jazz Singer (USA, Alan Crosland, 1927)
The Jew (Portugal-Brazil, Yom Tov Azulay, 1996)
Joshua Then and Now (Canada, Tod Kotcheff, 1985)
Judy Berlin (USA, Eric Mendelsohn, 1999)
Julia (USA, Fred Zinnemann, 1977)
Kadosh (Israel, Amos Gitai, 1999)
Kanal (Poland, Andrzej Wajda, 1957)

Kissing Jessica Stein (USA, Charles Herman-Wurmfeld, 2002)
Mr. Klein (France, Joseph Losey, 1976)
Lacombe, Lucien (France, Louis Malle, 1974)
Lansky (HBO Pictures, John McNaughton, 1999)
The Last Metro (France, Francois Truffaut, 1980)
Late Marriage (Israel, Dover Koshashvili, 2002)
Left Luggage (Belgium, Jeroen Krabbe,1998)
Lies My Father Told Me (Canada, Jan Kadar, 1975)
Little Odessa (USA, James Gray, 1995)
Lost in Yonkers (USA, Martha Coolidge, 1993)
Lovers in Minsk (German-Russian, Ulf von Mechow, 1994)
Madame Rosa (France, Moshe Mizrachi, 1977)
Man is a Woman (France, Jean. J. Zilberman, 1997)
Martha and I (German-Italy-France, Jiri Weiss, 1989)
Mendel (Norway, Alexander Rosler, 1998)
Meshuge (Germany, Dani Levi, 1999)
Monsieur Ibrahim (France, Francois Dupeyron, 2003)
My Mother's Courage (Germany, M. Verhoeven, 1996)
Nadia (Israel, Amnon Rubinstein, 1987)
The Nasty Girl (Germany, M. Verhoeven, 1990)
Nowhere in Africa (Germany, Caroline Link, 2001)
Operation Thunderbolt (Israel, M. Golan, 1977)
The Pawnbroker (USA, Sidney Lumet, 1965)
The Pianist (France, Roman Polanski, 2003)
Portnoy's Complaint (USA, Ernest Lehman, 1972)
A Price Above Rubies (USA, Boaz Yakin, 1998)
Private Benjamin (USA, Howard Zieff, 1980)
The Quarrel (Canada, Eli Cohen, 1992)
Quiz Show (USA, Robert Redford, 1994)
Radio Days (USA, Woody Allen, 1987)
Raid on Entebbe (USA, Irwin Kerschner, 1977)
The Revolt of Job (Hungary, Imre Gyongyossi, 1983)
Rosenstrasse (Germany, Margarethe von Trotta, 2004)
Russian Doll (Australia, Stavros Kazantzikis, 2000)
Sallach Shabati (Israel, E. Kishon, 1963)
Schindler's List (USA, Steven Spielberg, 1993)
School Ties (USA, Robert Mandel, 1992)
Shine (Australian, Scott Hicks, 1996)

Shop on Main Street (Czech, Jan Kadar, 1965)
Soleil (France-Germany, Roger Hanin, 1997)
Song of the Siren (Israel, Eytan Fox, 1994)
Sophie's Choice (USA, Alan J. Pakula, 1982)
The Substance of Fire (USA, Daniel Sullivan, 1996)
The Summer of Avia (Israel, Eli Cohen, 1988)
Tea with Mussolini (Franco Zeffirelli, 1999)
Tel Aviv-Berlin (Israel, Tzippi Trope, 1987)
Tel Aviv Stories (Nirit Yaron, 1992)
Tevie (USA, Maurice Schwartz, 1939)
Time of Favor (Israel, Joseph Cedar, 2000)
Three Days in April (Germany, Oliver Storz, 1995)
Train of Life (France, Radu Mihaileanu, 1998)
Triumph of the Spirit (USA, Robert Young, 1989)
Under the Domim Tree (Israel, Eli Cohen, 1995)
Victory at Entebbe (USA, Marvin Chomsky, 1976)
Les Violons du Bal (France, Michel Drach, 1973)
Voyages (France, Emmanuel Finkiel, 1999)
Yana's Friends (Israel, Daniel Syrkin, 1997)
Yentl (USA, Barbra Streisand, 1983)
Yom Yom (Israel, Amos Gitai, 1998)
Yossi and Jagger (Israel, Eytan Fox, 2002)

STUDIES IN HISTORY AND CRITICISM OF FILM

1a. Bert Cardullo, **Practical Film Criticism–An Enlightened Approach to Moviegoing, Volume I**
1b. Bert Cardullo, **Practical Film Criticism–An Enlightened Approach to Moviegoing, Volume II**
2. Hans Joachim Meurer, **Cinema and National Identity in a Divided Germany, 1979-1989: The Split Screen**
3. Del Jacobs, **Revisioning Film Traditions–The Pseudo-Documentary and the NeoWestern**
4. Phebe Davidson, **American Movies and their Cultural Antecedents in Literary Text**
5. Renata Jackson, **The Modernist Poetics and Experimental Film Practice of Maya Deren (1917-1961)**
6. Joachim Lembach, **The Standing of the German Cinema in Great Britain After 1945**
7. Josette Hollenbeck, **Aperçu culturel de films francophones**
8. William A. Drumin, **Thematic and Methodological Foundations of Alfred Hitchcock's Artistic Vision**
9. Russ Witcher, **A Textual Analysis of Movie Director Oliver Stone's** *Nixon*
10. Michael Taub, **Films About Jewish Life and Culture**